3-minute
CONSULTATIONS
with America's Greatest
PSYCHOTHERAPISTS

3-minute
CONSULTATIONS
with America's Greatest
PSYCHOTHERAPISTS

JASON ARONSON INC.
Northvale, New Jersey
London

Models used for illustrative purposes only.

This book was set in 12 pt. Garamond Book and printed and bound by Book-mart Press, Inc. of North Bergen, NJ.

Library of Congress Cataloging-in-Publication Data

3-minute consultations with America's greatest psychotherapists / compiled and edited by Jason Aronson.
    p. cm.
  Includes bibliographical references and appendix.
  ISBN 0-7657-0305-X
  1. Psychotherapy.   I. Title: Three minute consultations with America's greatest psychotherapists.   II. Aronson, Jason.

  RC408.5.A14 2000
  616.89'14—dc21

                                  00-046446

Printed in the United States of America on acid-free paper. For information and catalog write to Jason Aronson Inc., 230 Livingston Street, Northvale, New Jersey 07647-1726, or visit our website: www.aronson.com

Contents

PREFACE   xi

PART I: BASIC ISSUES

Starting Therapy
Thomas H. Ogden
The opening lines of
the analytic drama.

$\underline{1}$
3

Establishing the Fee
Peter S. Armstrong
The patient's unconscious
does not overlook the
therapist's actions.

$\underline{2}$
7

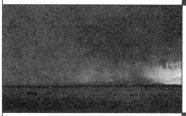

**Knowing a Good
Therapeutic Intervention
from a Bad One**
Stephen A. Appelbaum
An evocative empathic remark
can encourage elaboration.

$\underline{3}$
12

**Setting the Stage
for a Safe Voyage**
Jane S. Hall
The therapist has the same
obligation as the captain
of a ship: providing a
secure environment.

$\underline{4}$
17

**The Personality of
the Therapist**
Sheldon Roth
The pursuit of therapeutic
helpfulness.

$\underline{5}$
21

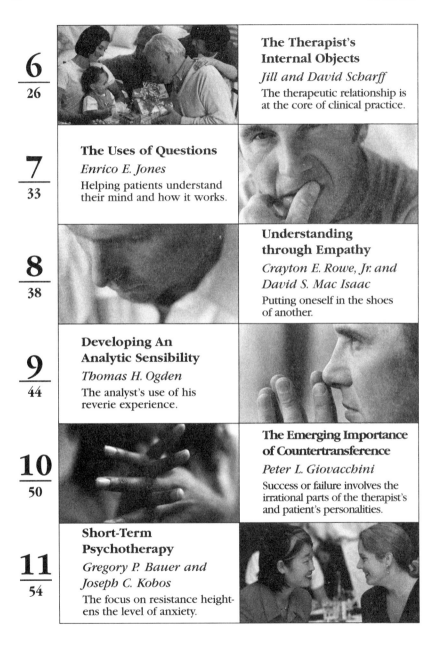

6
26

**The Therapist's
Internal Objects**

Jill and David Scharff

The therapeutic relationship is
at the core of clinical practice.

7
33

The Uses of Questions

Enrico E. Jones

Helping patients understand
their mind and how it works.

8
38

**Understanding
through Empathy**

*Crayton E. Rowe, Jr. and
David S. Mac Isaac*

Putting oneself in the shoes
of another.

9
44

**Developing An
Analytic Sensibility**

Thomas H. Ogden

The analyst's use of his
reverie experience.

10
50

**The Emerging Importance
of Countertransference**

Peter L. Giovacchini

Success or failure involves the
irrational parts of the therapist's
and patient's personalities.

11
54

**Short-Term
Psychotherapy**

*Gregory P. Bauer and
Joseph C. Kobos*

The focus on resistance heightens the level of anxiety.

Applying the Principles of Supportive Psychotherapy
Marc. H. Hollender and Charles V. Ford
Good intentions are not enough.
12
60

How Theory Helps the Therapist
Sanford Shapiro
Staying calm, even when confused, is half the battle.

13
64

Sexual Feelings about the Therapist
Glen O. Gabbard
Conflicting feelings of love and hate are inherent in therapy.
14
67

The Psychotherapist as Healer
T. Byram Karasu
The healer has no preset technique.

15
73

The Beginning of the End
Salman Akhtar
Achievements in therapy bring termination in sight.
16
78

The Limitations of Managed Care
Muriel Prince Warren
Focus is on quick, cost-effective change.

17
82

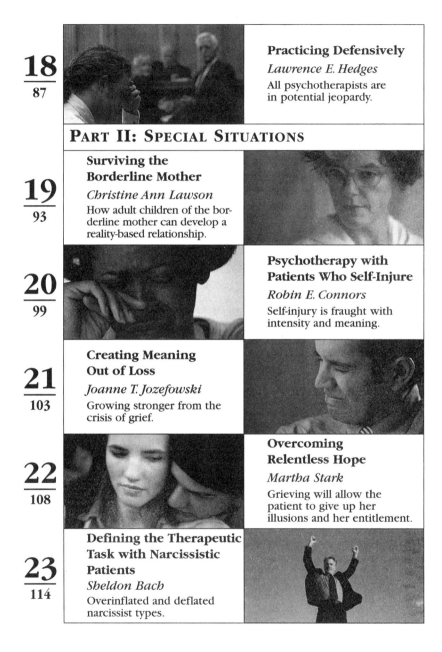

18
87

Practicing Defensively
Lawrence E. Hedges
All psychotherapists are
in potential jeopardy.

PART II: SPECIAL SITUATIONS

19
93

**Surviving the
Borderline Mother**
Christine Ann Lawson
How adult children of the bor-
derline mother can develop a
reality-based relationship.

20
99

**Psychotherapy with
Patients Who Self-Injure**
Robin E. Connors
Self-injury is fraught with
intensity and meaning.

21
103

**Creating Meaning
Out of Loss**
Joanne T. Jozefowski
Growing stronger from the
crisis of grief.

22
108

**Overcoming
Relentless Hope**
Martha Stark
Grieving will allow the
patient to give up her
illusions and her entitlement.

23
114

**Defining the Therapeutic
Task with Narcissistic
Patients**
Sheldon Bach
Overinflated and deflated
narcissist types.

Working with Borderline Patients

Otto Kernberg

Building ego strength through transference interpretations.

24
118

Treatment of Stress Response Syndromes

Mardi Horowitz

Attention to defensive coping and resistance to treatment is important.

25
122

Management of Severe Rejecting Behavior

Jeffrey Seinfeld

Facilitating the internalization of the therapist.

26
128

Psychotherapy with the Schizoid Patient

Philip Manfield

The schizoid seeks safety in emotional and interpersonal distance.

27
134

Combining Psychotherapy with Pharmacotherapy

Gerald L. Klerman et al.

Patient and therapist attitudes present problems.

28
139

Evaluation of Suicidal Potentiality

Robert E. Litman

Information about suicide emerges readily if asked for.

29
147

30
153

Use of the Telephone as a Transitional Space
Joyce K. Aronson

How do you work with a patient who refuses to come in to see you?

31
158

Treatment of Patients with Agoraphobia
Pat Sable

The therapist as a safe harbor.

32
163

Sexual Complaints Mask Our Deepest Wishes
Alan Bell

We must face and own the deepest versions of our reality.

33
168

Resolving Trouble in the Bedroom
Eva Margolies

Men with sexual problems and what women can do to help them.

34
173

Psychotherapy of the Psychopath
J. Reid Meloy

The more severe the psychopathic disturbance, the more likely psychotherapy will fail.

35
177

Assessing and Treating Criminals
Stanton E. Samenow

Avoiding both gullibility and cynicism.

183   **APPENDIX**

Preface

Competent therapy has the power to change us, to determine whether we go through life isolated and limited or with the emotional resources to maintain intimate relationships and respond creatively to life's inevitable crises. The growth of psychodynamic psychotherapy over recent decades is astonishing, and is evidence of its powerful impact on American culture and individual lives. This book shows why the surge in the number of patients has occurred, for it is about how the psychotherapist thinks: the force that makes such a compelling difference for us.

These essays, by the most prominent psychotherapists writing today, are taken from their seminal works. Part I covers basic issues that come up in every therapy. For example, the therapist walks into the waiting room and introduces himself to the new patient.

Does he ask, "Did you have trouble finding a parking place?", putting the patient at ease, or is he mostly silent, and if so, why? How is the fee discussed and what are the implications for the course of the therapy? How does a therapist shape those interventions that will be moving and memorable rather than dull and pedestrian? Patients often expect to be provided with explanations. How does the therapist focus instead on helping patients understand how their own minds work? How does the therapist respond to feelings of hate and erotic love that are so frequently expressed by patients?

Part II addresses specific situations. Some of the questions discussed are: How does one survive loss with renaissance of body, mind, and spirit? What is the meaning of self-injury such as cutting, burning, or head banging? How does a therapist approach grandiose narcissism? Why does grieving allow the patient to eventually let go of illusions? How does interpreting the borderline patient's distortion of the therapist's interventions build ego strength? What is the goal of treatment of stress response syndromes? How can the therapist effectively and tactfully ask about suicide? How can a woman's understanding of a man's impotence or premature ejaculation help him to recover?

This book is addressed to a wide audience of psychotherapists, counselors, psychiatrists, psychoanalysts, students of these disciplines, and laymen who are interested in psychotherapy. It's a book for browsing. Look through the table of contents and turn first to those essays that most arouse your interest.

—Jason Aronson

I

Basic
Issues

1

Starting Therapy

Thomas H. Ogden

A s with all other analytic meetings, the initial hour
begins in the waiting room. The patient is
addressed as Dr., Mr., or Ms., and the analyst introduces himself in kind. The paradox inherent in this
formal introduction is not lost to the patient: the
analytic relationship is one of the most formal and at
the same time one of the most intimate of human relationships. The formality is a reflection
of respect for the analysand and for the
analytic process. In addition, it is an
expression of the fact that the analyst
is not pretending to be, nor does he
aspire to be, the analysand's friend. (We
do not pay our friends to talk to us.) It
is therefore made clear from the outset
that the intimacy of the analytic rela-

*Thomas H.
Ogden*

tionship will be an intimacy in the context of formality.

Therapists early in their training often feel the impulse to "put the patient at ease" or "to act human" as they walk with the patient from the waiting room to the consulting room. For instance, a therapist attempting to ease the tension of the walk to the consulting room might say, "I hope you didn't have trouble finding a parking space. Parking is awful around here." To make such a comment is not a kind thing to do from the point of view of the analytic process. In fact, from the perspective being discussed, such a therapist would be considered rather unkind in several ways. First, he has communicated to the patient his unconscious feeling that the patient is an infant who has trouble making his way in a hostile world, and also the fact that the therapist feels guiltily responsible for not making the patient's life less difficult. Such a comment immedi-

ately puts the patient into the analyst's debt and puts pressure on him to return the "kindness"—that is, to help the analyst avoid feelings of discomfort. There is also a hint in the therapist's comment that he is not confident that the therapy he will offer the patient is worth the trouble to which the patient is going.

Furthermore, this sort of comment is an act of theft: it robs the patient of the opportunity to intro-duce himself to the analyst in the way that he con-sciously and unconsciously chooses. The patient has available to him an infinite number of ways of begin-ning the analytic discourse. His choice of the way he will go about doing this will be repeated by no other analysand. One must not deprive him of his opportu-nity to write the opening lines of his own analytic

---

This sort of comment is an act of theft: it robs the patient of the opportunity to introduce himself to the analyst in the way that he consciously and unconsciously chooses.

---

drama by burdening him with the analyst's own unconscious contents before he even sets foot in the consulting room. (There will be plenty of time for that later as the analyst inevitably becomes an unwitting actor in the patient's unconscious phantasies.)

Finally, a comment of the type being discussed mis-leads the patient about the nature of the analytic expe-rience. As analysts, we do not intend to relieve anxiety (our own or the patient's) through tension-reducing activity such as reassurances, gift-giving, and the like. Since maintaining psychological strain is not only something that we demand of ourselves, but also part of what we ask of the patient, it makes no sense to begin the analytic relationship with an effort at dissipating psychological strain. Whether or not the incident is ever spoken of again, the analysand unconsciously registers the fact that the analyst has granted himself license to handle his own anxiety by acting upon his countertransference feelings.

The patient brings to the first interview many questions and worries (usually unspoken) about what it means to be in analysis, what it means to be an analyst, and what it means to be an analysand. The analyst's attempts at answering these questions in the form of explanations of free association, the use of the couch, frequency of meetings, differences between psychotherapy and psychoanalysis, differences between "schools of psychoanalysis," and so on, are not only futile but invariably highly limiting of the patient's opportunity to present himself to the analyst in his own terms. The analyst's most eloquent explanation of what it means to be "in analysis" is to conduct himself as an analyst.

From *The Primitive Edge of Experience.* See page 185.

Thomas H. Ogden, M.D., teaches, supervises, and maintains a private practice of psychoanalysis in San Francisco.

> *The patient's unconscious does not overlook the therapist's actions.*

2

Establishing the Fee

Peter S. Armstrong

Setting the fee with a patient is a task that has been filled with anxiety and is the subject of much consideration in the literature. In my own work and in my work with therapists in supervision I have further confirmed the difficulties in this area, and yet setting the fee is essential to the work of psychotherapy. As Freud first noted, the therapist is responsible for handling matters of money in the same direct and open manner that will characterize the handling of all future matters.

Again, the formation of the transference and the nature of the stance of the therapist all require that fee setting be handled directly, with no difference from the way other matters are

Peter S.
Armstrong

handled. Otherwise the therapist has conveyed that some matters are too difficult to address and may be dismissed to an area of the unspoken. The topics to consider are: How does a therapist establish a fee even before discussing it with the patient? When and where in the first session (or phone call) is the fee introduced? Is the fee negotiable? How is it negotiated? Who "owns" the fee?

Setting one's fee is a somewhat arbitrary process, aside from the fee agreements made with insurance companies, Medicare, and managed-care contracts. I am describing here how to set fees for privately paying patients, those who are not involving a third-party payor. There is no true standard and no simple way to outline this process. One's fees clearly must be based on training and experience, the commonly charged rates in the community, and one's ability to attract

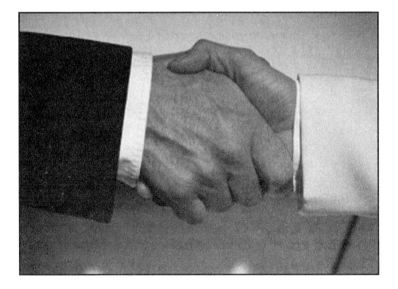

potential patients to his practice. There is no use holding out for one's "full fee" if no referrals call who can afford that fee. There is a business aspect to setting one's fee that has to do with the demand for one's services. Clearly, any student of human personality recognizes that some will overvalue their services and some will undervalue them. This is something that cannot be taught. It is a matter of personal self-understanding and personal ethics.

When is the fee set with the patient? If the therapist does not reduce her fee then there is no need to suggest in a phone call that the patient "talk about it" if that implies that the fee will be changed. There are many reasons and great value to talking about the fee, all of which are important material for the therapy. But

---

The process of discussing and arranging the fee offers many hints about the transference.

---

the willingness to negotiate a reduced rate or not must be made clear. Ethics codes increasingly demand that fees be stated even as early as in the first phone contact. These codes are attempts to constrain those therapists who use deceptive practices, luring a patient into a process the patient cannot afford, or with hidden charges that surprise that patient at some point. Such practices are unethical and counter to the process of analytic therapy. One cannot conduct a process requiring openness and honesty and begin it deceptively, whether about the fee or any other matter.

Today, amid the growing concerns about ethics and

laws affecting the therapist, I have heard lengthy talks about the honesty and ethics of various manipulations of fees charged to insurers. It is my opinion that it is hard to generate much concern for an industry that has manipulated therapists and their livelihoods without much apparent concern for ethics. However, the more important issue for the analytic therapist is the message conveyed to the patient by manipulation or dishonesty. One must question how these deceptions play into the transference and the call for honesty between the two individuals establishing a therapy relationship. Again, the basic concept is that the patient's unconscious does not overlook the therapist's actions.

The increasing demands on the therapist for concrete actions in the areas of disclosure and written contracts are disturbing because they tend to limit the many possible ways of entering into a relationship. Policies about how to set fees limit the therapist's observations and experience inherent in working out the fee with the patient. Whether or not one negotiates a fee, the process of discussing and arranging it offers many hints about the transference. These experiences and anxieties are best observed in a face-to-face session, not on the phone or as a patient reads a sheet of policies. My preference is to meet with all patients, regardless of their own perceived ability to pay, and then to explore the concerns about payment, the available resources, and any anxieties about the fee that might be addressed. If I choose to hold my fee at its full rate I state it at its full rate. I want to explore with the patient fantasies, expectations, and even the beginnings of negative transference. If I choose to reduce my fee I want that reduction to be for purposes of realistic considerations, following a careful review of the person's ability to pay. I do not believe that I can be the judge of someone's ability to pay. Individuals have all sorts of ways of determining the use of their money and I am not so arrogant as to believe that I can be the judge of how that ought to happen. Of course I value therapy and I wish to be paid for my services, so it is sometimes hard to see the other person's point of view.

From *Opening Gambits: The First Session of Psychotherapy.* See page 185.

Peter S. Armstrong, Ph.D., a clinical psychologist and psychoanalyst, is currently on the faculty of the Oregon Psychoanalytic Society and Institute and the Northwest Center for Psychoanalysis.

An evocative empathic remark can encourage elaboration.

3

Knowing a Good Therapeutic Intervention from a Bad One

Stephen A. Appelbaum

Most psychotherapists know a good intervention from a bad one—whether it is moving, persuasive, and memorable, or dull, pedestrian, and inconsequential. They may, however, be much less sure of why it is one way or another and of the best way to make the delivery of their own interventions more effective.

The hospital billing department alerted the therapist that his patient had not paid his psychotherapy bill for the past three months.

Stephen A. Appelbaum

T: I understand that you haven't paid your psychotherapy bill for some time.

P: Oh, it's been hard to catch up this summer. Trying to pay a little here and a little there (pause) especially since losing my job. (Pause.) I've been paying what I can, but I know I'm behind.

T: It really seems like a dark cloud hovering over your head.

P: And I don't know how to get out of it! The money that we put aside is dwindling, and I'm beginning to think that it won't be easy to get another position.

The therapist's "dark cloud" image evocatively speaks the language of depression. "Hanging over your

head" speaks the language of anticipatory anxiety, perhaps bordering on panic ("I don't know how to get
out of it"). The therapist's resonance at that moment
seems to have encouraged the patient toward enlarg-
ing the meaning to him of his predicament, for the
patient adds a dwindling theme. His choice of "dwindling" suggests that he equates his financial impotence
with sexual impotence. The ongoing gerund form suggests that he feels that his dwindling is steadily getting
worse. He begins to worry about a complete collapse,
an inability to find a solution ("another position").
The therapist should be able to continue the resonance thus established with the patient with some
such remark as, "You seem not only to feel sad and

---

*There is a difference between an unevocative, gray,
forgettable blip on one's sensory screen and a profound
experience that embodies nuances of the present,
reminders of the past, and intimations of the future.*

---

regretful, but deeply worried. Perhaps your difficulty
paying your bill right now lights up a lifelong worry
about being the man you would like to be—capable,
a problem-solver, potent."

This brief passage pithily illustrates how an evocative empathic remark can encourage elaboration,
derivatives, and the patient's own evocativeness.
Instead of referring to the ominous "dark cloud" feeling, the therapist could have gone further in the bill-
collecting mode, or focused on the patient's "guilt" and
"depression" using those overused clinical words, or
countless other interventions, ranging from dull to

disastrous. Instead the therapist and the patient took steps toward a cloudless sky.

There are sunsets, and there are sunsets, Some dusks, the sun just quietly slips away. Other dusks, one stares at the changing sky transfixed, or runs for a camera. We are surrounded by such variations in color, drama, and impact. And like fish who seem unaware of the water because of its omnipresence, we tend to overlook the varying degrees by which our surroundings capture our imaginations and move us.

I call these variations in emotional and sensory impact "evocativeness." If there were such a thing as a meter to measure evocativeness, we could put the meter on anything and get a reading, an indication of the thing's capacity to evoke a response. Sometimes the capacity is inherent, as in a purple orchid, a redo-

lent stew, the luminous light of an eye. Sometimes evocativeness is enlisted. This is true for the arts, and for the artistic, creative aspect of psychotherapy. A high reading on the evocativeness meter, for a speech in the theater as for the delivery of an interpretation, indicates the difference between an unevocative, gray, forgettable blip on one's sensory screen and a profound experience that embodies nuances of the

---

You may remember and learn from the memory of an evocative comment for the rest of your life.

---

present, reminders of the past, and intimations of the future. That movement on the evocative meter reflects the amazing amalgam of feeling and thought that *communicates* rather than just communicates.

Picture yourself, at the end of a play or movie, making the journey from your seat out to the lobby, then into the outside world. After some theater performances or films, you will have forgotten the experience by the time you hit the sidewalk. After others you revel in the pity and terror of it all, are haunted by reminders the next few days and nights, and may remember and learn from that memory for the rest of your life.

From *Evocativeness: Moving and Persuasive Interventions in Psychotherapy.* See page 185.

Stephen A. Appelbaum, M.D., was in the private practice of psychoanalysis, psychotherapy, and diagnostic testing, after many years on the staff of the Menninger Clinic in Topeka, Kansas.

> *The therapist has the same obligation as the captain of a ship: providing a secure environment.*

Setting the Stage for a Safe Voyage

Jane S. Hall

Psychoanalytically oriented psychotherapy is a journey inward. Travelers are always anxious to some degree. When the vehicle of transport seems safe and sturdy, and the pilot or captain impresses the passenger with her expertise and confidence, the traveler can relax to some extent. The therapist has the same obligation: providing a safe and secure environment for travel.

Many people who come to a therapist have felt betrayed early in life and therefore do not trust easily, if at all. Since the unique relationship between patient and therapist that evolves over time provides new opportunities for trusting, setting the stage is very important. The therapist's attitude of

Jane S. Hall

17

respect, patience, and benevolent curiosity combined with her confidence in the analytic process is what impresses the patient and permits her to stay in treatment. The persistent durability and constancy of the therapist and her functions present the patient with a new reality, one that holds the potential for reviewing and experiencing the calamities of life in a new way. Differentiation becomes safe. Separations become bearable. Competition becomes acceptable. Feelings of effectiveness become more rewarding than feelings of omnipotence and grandiosity. Experiences of success and failure can exist side by side and do not cancel each other out. Closeness and intimacy become possible.

How do we set the stage for the deeper work that needs to be done? How do we create a safe environment? How do we pass the tests?

1. By having an inner conviction that each person has a unique story to tell, and respecting his or her way of relating it;
2. By listening carefully and following what the patient says attentively so that we can make connections and interpretations when appropriate;
3. By being confident that the long-term process of working through is necessary and possible for the patient to resume development and diminish conflict;
4. By being nonjudgmental, nonintrusive, and open-minded;
5. By listening for strength as well as for pathology, and not letting premature diagnoses or diagnostic labels cloud the picture;
6. By being respectful of the patient's pace and autonomy;
7. By being firm and flexible when either is appropriate, and learning how to know when to be which;
8. By listening with respect, and by being comfortable not knowing the answers—or even the questions sometimes;
9. By encouraging and protecting the patient's curiosity and capacity for self-reflection;
10. By not burdening the patient with personal information and opinions;
11. By remembering that no two cases are alike, and that each patient creates her own theory (not fitting the patient into the theory);
12. By setting the conditions of treatment such as fee, payment, vacation policy, and missed session policy in the consultation phase so as to clear the way for

work without distraction;

13. By remembering that growth and not cure is the goal;

14. By being consistent, reliable, calm, and benevolently curious;

15. By providing an atmosphere of trust, safety, and confidentiality.

From *Deepening the Treatment.* See page 186.

Jane S. Hall, M.S.W., a member of the New York Freudian Society, is in private practice in New York City.

5

The Personality of the Therapist

Sheldon Roth

The therapist seasoned in the art and science of psychotherapy knows that this skill has been garnered not only through intensive study of patients but through profound intensive self-study as well. Our early training fashions for us objective, scientific glasses through which we view the patient. We are taught to recognize signs, symptoms, patterns, and clinical syndromes, all of which take place in an external reality—another person—quite separate from ourselves. By assuming the role of therapist, we are unexpectedly thrust into a novel, organic relationship with this tidy objective compilation of clinical labels, the patient. Suddenly, or gradually, there comes an aware-

Sheldon Roth

ness that our own signs, symptoms, patterns, and characteristic ways of being have a realistic impact on the therapeutic process. Subjective intuition and empathy, which depend on our personal self-awareness and self-mastery, are indispensable adjuncts to objective knowledge, if we are able to be clinically attuned to the patient, whose unpredictable emotional waters demand that we sink or swim in surprising new ways.

The neophyte therapist, as well as the experienced one, is often stunned by the extent of the hostility with which good intentions are met. If any one element is underestimated in approaching a career as a psychotherapist, it is the amount of hostility and rejection that will be one's lot in the pursuit of therapeutic helpfulness. A great threat to personal integrity and self-worth will come about through open

rejection of one's most heartfelt efforts to be of use, the sharing of intuitions with the patient, and the provision of great patience and forbearance; the patient may still, in spite of all these, declare the therapist inadequate, short of the mark, and uncaring. The more regressed or disturbed a patient is, the more destructive the hostility will be. All but the most far-sighted of therapists never consider, when choosing therapy as a career, the major share of daily experience this open hostility will consume.

An immense sense of personal security about one's value and motives is needed to weather patients' emotional storms and these assaults against one's self-esteem. Unfortunately, this sense of personal value will not be in great supply at the onset of the therapist's training or even during the initial years of clinical practice.

If any one element is underestimated in approaching a career as a psychotherapist, it is the amount of hostility and rejection that will be one's lot in the pursuit of therapeutic helpfulness.

The good therapist is also a realist. Professional self-worth exists only when clinical experience has proven that one possesses skill. During the early years of practice, it is of the highest importance that one has good training and continues to work with supervisors and seek the sustaining wisdom of their own successes and failures. Indeed, even therapists with many years of experience will find ways to continue sharing this onus of self-doubt and confusion through study groups, attentive work at professional meetings, and the reading of professional journals for confirmations, comparisons, and learning.

Although the role of psychotherapist tends to attract those who feel deep fascination with the lives and experiences of others, psychotherapy is a profession that paradoxically engenders loneliness. Only a scant portion of one's daily work can be communicated to others, due partly to ethical considerations, limitations of time in sharing case material, and fears of acting out some unbidden countertransference. Equally significant is the regressive dreamlike quality of the intense psychotherapeutic experience, which, like the nocturnal dream, defies full verbal description. In addition, the listening therapist is suffused with such a barrage of instinctual stimulation from the patient's material that a subtle, sanity-saving suppression and repression is put into effect almost as the material unfolds.

As I begin to hint at the tidal onrush of difficulty for the therapist, it may be helpful to look at those qualities that must already exist in the personality of the therapist who enters this uncertain domain. Frieda Fromm-Reichmann, a therapeutic talent greatly admired for her work with severely disturbed and regressed patients, was asked what was most important in psychotherapy. She stated: "If I were asked to answer this question in one sentence, I would reply, the psychotherapist must be able to listen." Her simple comment reflects on a personal quality that is quite complex, a condensation and surface manifestation of many elements of personality.

One therapist who understood some of the roots

of his pleasure in listening explained:

> My mother had no patience with teaching. . . .
> When I was young, for example, she tried to teach
> me to play golf. Each time I'd make a mistake she'd
> fly into a rage, and often couldn't contain herself.
> She'd hit me on the arm or the head! . . . Finally, she
> got totally disgusted, gave up on me, and said, "Let
> your father do it!"

I have infinite patience with my patients. . . . I can listen, listen, listen! They can have all the time they want. . . . I know what it feels like to have someone exasperated, full of rage, and impulsive. . . . I will do anything not to be like that with someone.

From *Psychotherapy: The Art of Wooing Nature.* See page 186.

Sheldon Roth, M.D., is a training and supervising analyst at the Psychoanalytic Institute of New England East (PINE) and in the private practice of psychiatry and psychoanalysis.

6

The Therapist's
Internal Objects

Jill and David Scharff

As individual therapists and psychoanalysts, we
work alone with one patient at a time. Yet we are
embedded in a matrix of other relationships, and so
are they. An internal group accompanies us, hindering
and helping us, as we work each day. It combines
experience, perception, memory, feeling, and thought
in our psychic structure, at various levels: first, our
internal images of the people in our
household, based on our history
together and our recent interactions;
second, the internal characters who
travel from the past with us; third, our
accumulated clinical experience with
previous patients; fourth, our present
group of patients; and, last, the group
of ideas that we use to make sense of

*Jill and David
Scharff*

our therapeutic experience. Our self-analysis of this internal group's effect on the way that we relate to each patient is fundamental to the object relations therapy approach.

We begin each day in the company of our internal objects. We take them into our office. We bring with us our internal versions of our spouse, children and parents, our professional colleagues, supervisors, friends, and enemies. We carry with us, in our inner world, our memories of previous patients, some of them gratifying, some puzzling, and some of them abandoning objects. We are filled with our experiences with the patients of that day. We may be taunted, amused, exhausted, uplifted, bored, and intrigued. At every level, these are the objects of our dreams, our hopes and fears, our preoccupations and musings. Then we have the thoughts that help us through

to understanding, as new ideas, triggered by working with this man or that woman, build upon old ideas, sometimes transforming them.

Like us, individual patients bring into our office an internal group based on the people in their lives. As patients tell us at length about their conflicts with husbands and wives, mothers and fathers, brothers and sisters, uncles and aunts, children and grandchildren, friends and enemies, we see the contours of this internal group emerging. Patients talk seriously about the bosses and employees they like to work with and those they hate. They tell us about the friends with whom they relax. They may refer to the loss of a previous therapist and expect us to be as wonderful, or fear that we will be equally useless. They roam over

---

Our self-analysis of this internal group's effect on the way that we relate to each patient is fundamental to the object relations therapy approach.

---

their relationships—of the past, the present, and the unknown future. As therapy progresses, the patient's individual internal group presents itself as a living reality that interacts with our own internal group, based on our personal and family experience and current clinical experience with patients.

As we meet the patients one by one, they build up our daily experience of work and form a clinical group. As we listen, we receive a cast of hundreds who jostle for space, find something to identify with inside us, and click with myriad parts of us that accept or reject them. Present patients join the group of family and friends in being the stuff of our internal worlds, the people to whom we relate in intimate ways, with whom or against whom we identify, through whom our own hopes and fears are fulfilled and frustrated. They do not know each other, but they form a group in our minds nevertheless, and each one has a place in that internal group.

And so it goes through the day. I (D.E.S.) have a brief break, refill my coffee up, take the message from voice mail to call the tutor of an adolescent patient who drags her feet at finishing her work and getting to school on time. I glance at the newspaper: "Mass Suicide of 39 Cult Members." Incredulous and overwhelmed with the horror of what happened in that group, I find my spirits sinking.

I'm relieved to be pulled out of the gloom when the bell rings just exactly on time for Alma Schultz. Mrs. Schultz always comes just on time—the most efficient patient I've had in a long time. She gets things done, but her efficiency, which lets her manage an ambitious professional life and a family, hides great sadness and a conviction that no one knows how bad and destructive she is, and how little her life is worth. I think of the suicide I just read about, and hope that she is never drawn toward death. I like her, and admire her, but last week she told me that she has felt from the beginning that she irritated me, that I barely put up with her. How can someone about whom I feel so positively be so convinced I do not like her? I am far from understanding her. Then I realize that I am having evoked in me parts of her that she gets rid of: while I identify her with the exciting object, she identifies the rejecting object with me. Bridging this distance in my sense of her helps me, during the next session, to appreciate and communicate my understanding of Mrs. Schultz's distance from herself.

As Mrs. Schultz leaves, I see Eric Hamburg in the waiting room, sitting restlessly at the edge of his chair, his leather jacket across his lap, its collar held tight in his clenched hand. He is from a poor family where his uneducated father was physically abusive to him. His anxiety transmits itself to me and joins with the lingering sadness I feel for Mrs. Schultz. I move beyond that past hour to think about Mr.

How can someone about whom I feel so positively be so convinced I do not like her?

Hamburg. Earlier this week, I told him that his self-defeating symptoms were his way of beating himself up to maintain allegiance to the abusive father that he longed for and loved. I said that he kept the physically abusive relationship to his father alive through verbal outbursts at his wife and children. He looked as if I had hit him. Today Mr. Hamburg reminds me of a British coal worker, cleaned up to ask a favor from the boss. Perhaps in the transference Mr. Hamburg has an unspoken longing for me, as he has for his father, and only when I "hit" him could I become aware of it.

Patients tell us about their lives—some interesting, some mundane—in narratives that hold our attention and may move us deeply, although we do not respond by sharing similar narratives of our own. They leave imperceptible traces or deep footprints through the years. They interact in our minds, sometimes quite openly as they preoccupy us or appear in a dream, stir a fantasy, or create a connection with something we have read.

Patients do more than cross paths in the waiting room. They form a group that assembles only in the mind of the therapist. As they interact with each other and with us, they also, to some degree, comment on our competence. Their success and growth fosters our conviction that our form of therapy offers repair; their difficulty erodes our sense of goodness. Even when the patients do not talk to each other, and we do not talk about them, the group of internal objects based on them comprises an internal teaching seminar, a promotions committee, a reference group for our well-being, and an inner circle of privileged communication.

We live in, among, and through our patients. We make mistakes with them, set things right with them. Although they are not the only members of our internal worlds, professionally they are the most important ones. They bump shoulders (without seeing or being seen) with our colleagues, supervisors, teachers, and students. They resemble aspects of our children, parents, and spouses, and like them are subject to our affection, discomfort, envy, admiration, or thank-God-it's-not-me reactions. They are with us every day, near or far, around and within.

In object relations therapy, we focus on the individual patient's internal group and its effect on the patient's perceptions of us, as well as their effect on us, their way of using us as objects, and their experience of us. We are not simply monitoring the relationship to maintain a good alliance. We are not avoiding confrontation or empathic failures. We are there to provide a space for thinking and feeling. We are there as objects for use. We use whatever occurs in the laboratory of the therapeutic relationship as a shared experience for examination. In summary, the therapeutic relationship is now at the core of clinical practice.

From *Object Relations Individual Therapy.* See page 186.

Jill Savege Scharff, M.D., is Co-Director of the International Institute of Object Relations Therapy and Clinical Professor of Psychiatry at Georgetown University.

David E. Scharff, M.D., is Co-Director of the International Institute of Object Relations Therapy and Clinical Professor of Psychiatry at Georgetown University.

7

The Uses
of Questions

Enrico E. Jones

Patients often approach therapy with the expectation that the therapist will relatively easily comprehend why they feel as they do, and then deliver transformative explanations. They consciously or unconsciously hope that the therapist will provide knowledge, resolve conflicts and dilemmas, and advise them about how to conduct their life. Most patients must learn that self-understanding, as opposed to received wisdom, will be the means by which they are able to change and sustain their change. The foremost goal of analytic therapies is to help patients understand how they think, how they feel, the nature of their relations to others—in short, to understand their mind

*Enrico E.
Jones*

33

and how it works. Much of what the patient does in
therapy will be in the form of learning to perceive,
express, and reflect on experience. The patient's self-
observation is a necessary precondition for a change
process to occur. Some basic techniques for developing these capacities in the patient include questions.

Let us consider the uses of questions in analytic
therapies. The difficulty in discussing questions as a
technique is that as a rhetorical form or grammatical
construction, questions can be put to many uses, and
potentially have many different connotations to
patients. Questions can in themselves be interpretations. A common use of questions is, of course, to
discover more about the patient's difficulties and to
clarify the nature of problems. Questions may also
serve as a means of inviting the patient's curiosity, or
to point the patient toward a domain of inquiry that

the therapist thinks might be productive. However, there have been concerns among some psychoanalytic clinicians about the role of questions. Questions may, for example, implicitly require the patient to submit to the therapist's interests or agenda. They may also mask the introduction of ideas, or even criticisms, and contain suggestions.

Questions, like all therapist actions, can be thought about in terms of interaction structures. For example, if a patient is passive and does not easily reveal much about himself, the therapist may feel prodded to ask questions. Over time, the therapist may find himself reflexively accepting the role the patient is forcing on him, falling into a pattern of taking over the therapy

---

It is impossible to know what patients' experience will be of a question posed by the therapist.

---

sessions and guiding the patient with a series of questions. This would constitute an interaction structure, a way in which therapist and patient relate to one another that likely has important meanings. The questions may gratify the patient's need to evoke interest and concern, or represent a way to avoid thinking about himself. For the therapist, the routine of questioning might express a need to be seen as an authority, or mask impatience or criticism of the patient's passivity. The meanings of such an interaction structure, for which questions are verbal "markers," should be explicitly recognized and understood.

It is impossible to know what patients' experience

will be of a question posed by the therapist. Their reactions must be considered within the subjective and intersubjective experiences of a particular moment in treatment. Questions may allow one patient to experience the therapist as involved and responsive, but lead another to experience the therapist as intrusive and controlling. In general, the role of questions as a technique in psychotherapy is best understood in the interactive field created by therapist and patient.

There are a few generally agreed-upon guidelines about the kinds of questions therapists should *not* ask. Therapists should refrain from asking questions out of self-interest. They should not, for example, ask a patient the least traffic-congested route to a destination, or to repeat the name of a good hotel. A somewhat more complex example is refraining from asking a foreign-born patient about cultural practices out of a sense of personal interest or curiosity. Such questions can be easily rationalized as a means of furthering our understanding of the patient. The point here is that therapists can experience the urge to question for a variety of reasons, and should try to be aware of their motives. Less experienced therapists sometimes ask questions out of a sense of not knowing what to do. Anxiety or difficulty tolerating silence can also be motives for asking patients questions. It is important for patients to have some uninterrupted silence for thoughtful reflection.

Another guiding principle might be to ask questions not necessarily for the purpose of obtaining an answer, or to evoke a particular reaction, but rather to stimulate further thought. It is often useful to anticipate what the question will precipitate in the experience of the patient, and what the patient will think the therapist is trying to evoke. The patient's experience of a question can often be surmised from the nature of the interaction patterns dominant at that particular point in the treatment.

One long-standing reservation about the use of questions among psychoanalytic clinicians is the possibility that questions may hamper the free-association process, requiring the patient to rely upon more rational, reality-oriented forms of cognition. However, it cannot be assumed that a question forecloses or opens the possibilities for exploration. Everything depends on the experience of the question for the patient in the context of an ongoing interaction with the therapist. Similarly, it cannot be assumed that questions represent a demand on the patient to accommodate to the therapist's interests. Contemporary two-person or intersubjective approaches remind us that the therapist's agenda cannot avoid emerging just because the therapist is silent or avoids questions; the therapist's interests and priorities are continually communicated both directly and indirectly. Exploring the meaning of the therapist's question to the patient, as with any other aspect of the therapist's activity or presence, may lead to new understanding or awareness.

From *Therapeutic Action: A Guide to Psychoanalytic Therapy.* See page 187.

Enrico E. Jones, Ph.D., is Professor of Psychology at the University of California, Berkeley, and a practicing psychoanalyst in Berkeley.

8

Understanding through Empathy

Crayton E. Rowe, Jr. and David S. Mac Isaac

How do we go about sensing the inner life of another person? Perhaps the familiar phrase, "to put oneself into the shoes of another," best describes this process and most accurately captures what Kohut means by "experience-near." Simply stated, the analyst attempts to experience as closely as possible what the patient is experiencing (an approximation). Let us consider this normal human process as it occurs regularly among people.

Each of us has an ongoing, continuous flow of inner experiences. These may include our experience of a certain event or situation, such as a rainy day or a difficult task. They may include our experience of another person's experiencing an event or situation. Our experiences also include our own experience of ourselves. And finally, they may also include our experience of others experiencing us as we experience them. This intersubjective process is one that occurs whenever human beings interact.

Let us use a simple example. Your female friend purchases a new car with all the extras such as air-conditioning, stereo sound system, sun roof, and power windows. She is particularly thrilled with herself and her purchase because she has shopped around and feels she has gotten the best buy. She is excited to show you. In turn, you have a series of impressions that are taken in with your senses that include a total experience of the car itself and of your friend's experience of her new car. You see the glistening new paint and hear the quiet hum of the engine. You feel the plush upholstery and smell the scent of fresh leather. At the same time, you experience your friend's pride in her

new purchase and her boastfulness as she describes how she was able to get a good buy. In turn, your friend may experience your being less excited than she is about her purchase. She, in turn, begins to feel some disappointment.

Though this intersubjective flow of experiences may sound complicated in its description, it is a process that goes on in every human interaction. Unless one is a trained clinician, it is not something we think about consciously because our minds have the capacity to perceive and synthesize without our conscious awareness.

Returning to the clinical setting, the analyst's own focus remains consistently upon what the patient is

---

Empathic immersion into the patient's experience focuses the analyst's attention upon what it is like to be the subject rather than the target of the patient's wishes and demands.

---

experiencing. This encompasses not only the moment-to-moment experiences of the patient but also the continuous flow of these experiences over time. Kohut refers to the attunement to this continuous flow of moment-to-moment experiences as *prolonged immersion* or as long-term *empathic immersion* in the psychological field. Empathic immersion into the patient's experience focuses the analyst's attention upon what it is like to be the subject rather than the target of the patient's wishes and demands. The following brief vignettes exemplify this important distinction.

Mr. S., a middle-aged man with a history of work problems, rushed into the consulting room after tossing his rain-soaked coat upon one of the analyst's newly upholstered office chairs. The analyst was concerned about his chair and annoyed by his patient's apparent lack of consideration. Initially viewing himself as the target of the patient's unconscious projections, the analyst interpreted the act as an expression of displaced anger. Mr. S., in turn, became apologetic and immediately removed his coat from the chair.

Realizing in the moment that he had responded to the patient's behavior (outside the patient's experience), the analyst shifted his attention to what Mr. S. was experiencing and away from himself as a target.

From this "experience-near" vantage point, he recognized that his patient felt misunderstood and hurt by the interpretation. The analyst communicated this understanding and, furthermore, came to understand that Mr. S. had entered the office so excited and so preoccupied with his desire to share his good news about a job promotion that he had thoughtlessly tossed his coat. In turn, being understood allowed Mr. S. to arrive at an important awareness: namely, that his excitement in wishing to be recognized led, at times, to careless and inappropriate behavior that other people sometimes found offensive.

The following vignette illustrates another example of a patient feeling misunderstood when an intervention was made outside his experience.

> During the middle phase of his treatment, a young man in his late teens would initiate each session with a quip or a joke. At the start of one particular session, as the patient glanced over at a plant hanging by the window, he laughingly commented, "What kind of plant is that, it looks sick!" The analyst, viewing himself as the target of the remark, interpreted the patient's comment as an expression of aggression displaced from him as the transference object onto the patient's rage against his father, which had recently emerged in the treatment. The patient felt hurt by the intervention and countered by explaining that his jokes were not attacks but were, rather, his way of being close. He said, "I see these jokes as my being more comfortable

with you and wanting to relate to you like a friend. This may sound strange, but this is the way I am with all my good friends and they with me. We're always kidding one another."

As the analyst shifted his attention to the "experience-near" vantage point, he came to a new understanding of the meaning that joking held for his patient. Rather than an attack on the analyst as "target," his joking was a means of achieving closeness. In time the patient was able to uncover how his joking was a way of maintaining a relationship with his cold and distant father.

From *Empathic Attunement: The "Technique" of Psychoanalytic Self Psychology.* See page 187.

Crayton E. Rowe, Jr., M.S.W,. is a Training Analyst for The New York Freudian Society and maintains a private practice in psychoanalysis and psychotherapy in New York City.

David S. Mac Isaac, Ph.D., is a founding member of the New York Institute for Psychoanalytic Self Psychology and maintains a private practice in psychotherapy and psychoanalysis in Englewood, New Jersey.

9

Developing an Analytic Sensibility

Thomas H. Ogden

The development of an analytic sensibility centrally involves the enhancement of the analyst's capacity to feel in a visceral way the alive moments of an analytic session, to be able to hear that a word or a phrase has been used, has been "made anew" in an interesting, unexpected way; to notice that a patient's glance in the waiting room feels coy or apologetic or steamy; to sense that a message left on one's answering machine feels dangerously, and yet alluringly mysterious; to experience in a bodily way that a period of silence in the hour feels like lying in bed with one's spouse whom one has loved for many years, but who now feels like a stranger.

Thomas H. Ogden

In my efforts to make use of my experience in the analytic relationship, an enormous difficulty presents itself: much if not most of my feeling experience while with an analysand is not initially a part of my conscious awareness. It is here that one of the fundamental paradoxes of analytic practice lies. In order to do analytic work, the analyst must be able to experience and talk with himself (in as full a way as possible) about what it feels like being with the patient; and yet, for the most part, these experiences are unconscious. The analyst is initially, and for quite a long time, more "lived by" these predominantly unconscious feelings, than he is the author of a set of thoughts, feelings, and sensations that he experiences as his own creations and can name for himself. A good deal of my work as an analyst involves the effort to transform my experience of "I-ness" (myself as unselfconscious subject) into an experience of "me-ness" (myself as object of analytic scrutiny).

Reverie, like the manifest content of dreams, is an aspect of conscious experience that is intimately connected with unconscious experience. One must struggle to "hold onto" one's reverie experience before it is "reclaimed" by the unconscious. This struggle is not only a struggle with the forces of repression, but because our reverie experience is so large a part of our almost invisible background sense of self, it is equally a struggle with the wish/need for "the privacy of the self." A reverie that has at one moment seemed fully available to conscious awareness will frequently at the next moment seem to have "disappeared" leaving only a non-specific residue of feeling in its wake.

Reverie, like the manifest content of dreams,
is an aspect of conscious experience that is intimately
connected with unconscious experience.

Thus, the analyst's use of his reverie experience is in my view a central component of analytic technique. Perhaps the following brief (highly schematized) clinical vignette may be of value in conveying something of the experience of reverie and its role in the analytic process.

In a recent hour, an analysand, Mr. W., told me with a great deal of intensity of feeling, how much it frightened him to be as "mentally out of control" as he is. Mr. W. had been twice married and twice divorced, each time leaving his former wife with children from whom he felt quite estranged. He said that I was the only person to whom he had revealed the full extent of his "craziness." As Mr. W. was speaking, my mind "wandered" to thoughts about my upcoming 50th birthday. I recalled a recent conversation with a friend in which I had half-jokingly said that I was "handling" turning 50 by refusing to believe it. The "joke" in retrospect felt like a self-conscious attempt to be witty. I seemed to be trying too hard and felt embarrassed as I went over the conversation in my mind. As I re-focused my attention on what Mr. W. was say-ing, I attempted to consider my reverie in the context of what was going on in the analytic relationship. After a while, I said to Mr. W. that I had the impression that, while I thought he felt genuinely frightened of the degree to which he feels crazy and out of control, I had the sense that at other times (and perhaps even now), he succeeds in making that sense of himself so unreal to himself that he does not believe it to be a part of who he is. Mr. W. was silent for a few moments and then said (in a way that was noticeably less pressured than before) that when he talks about analysis as if it were "an elective thing" for him, his "craziness" feels like something from the distant past or maybe even something happening to somebody else whom he knows well, but is not entirely him. "It's not that I really think of it as another person, but it doesn't feel like me."

In this clinical situation, I was able to make use of

a seemingly unrelated set of feelings and thoughts that I "recalled" during the session with Mr. W. Thoughts and feelings about my upcoming 50th birthday had occurred with a number of patients that I was seeing during that period. However, in each instance, the images, thoughts, feelings, and sensations that were generated were contextualized by, and strongly reflected, the specific qualities of the conscious and unconscious constructions that were most pressing with each individual patient. In the session described, it seemed to me that the reverie concerning

---

The illusion of playfulness in the "joke" served to disguise the strained, manic defenses.

---

the "joke" about "handling" the birthday by refusing to believe it reflected my reliance on a form of splitting and omnipotent thinking that were designed to protect me from directly naming and fully experiencing the pain associated with the event.

Moreover, the cavalier quality of the "performance" seemed to claim victory over both my own feelings and the passage of time. The illusion of playfulness in the "joke" served to disguise the strained, manic defenses that I was using in order not to experience the sadness and fear that were for me associated with turning 50. It had been only a few days prior to her fiftieth birthday that my closest friend had learned of the wide metastatic spread of her breast cancer. The feeling of embarrassment in my reverie (the awareness of my transparent effort to be clever) seems to me in retrospect to have been a reflection of my feeling of embarrassment about my wish to evade fear associated with the recognition and acknowledgment of my own mortality (which had become all too real) and the deep sadness I felt in connection with the death of a friend. I was only dimly aware of this aspect of my experience at the juncture in the analysis being described.

From *Conversations at the Frontier of Dreaming.* See page 188.

Thomas H. Ogden, M.D., teaches, supervises, and maintains a private practice of psychoanalysis in San Francisco.

> *Success or failure involves the irrational parts of the therapist's and patient's personalities.*

10

The Emerging Importance of Countertransference

Peter L. Giovacchini

Clinicians are becoming increasingly aware that treatment success or failure is a complex issue that stresses the irrational parts of both the therapist's and the patient's personalities. Although it was accepted that the treatment course would vary, it was expected that the well-conducted analysis would follow a somewhat predictable sequence. The technical tool of free association would help stimulate a manageable regression, bringing to the forefront specific defenses and resistances that would contribute to the shape of transference projections. After resistances and defenses were analyzed, the oedipal constellation would be reenacted and the analyst would

Peter L. Giovacchini

become a parental figure, a situation often referred to as the *transference neurosis*. The termination period of treatment would begin with the resolution and working through of the transference neurosis.

As I listened to candidates presenting their control cases during clinical seminars, it became clear that the impassive, neutral analyst—or in this case the impassive, neutral future analyst—was a myth rather than a reality. Candidates struggled with their own feelings as well as those of their patients. Perhaps this struggle could be explained by their lack of professional maturity, but many senior analysts were able to empathize with their students and recounted similar episodes in their practices. The orderly course of treatment, such a desirable objective, also seemed to be on the far horizons of our clinical experience.

The measuring instrument—the therapist—has a

life of his own. Therapists are not impassive or neutral if they wish to treat the majority of patients who seek their services. Our attitudes about the analyst's technical and emotional participation in the treatment process must be constantly scrutinized. Much of the professional literature is directed toward questions that stress how we perceive and react toward patients. What was once considered undesirable is now in the forefront of clinical assessments. Countertransference has become a meaningful counterpart to transference projections as the essence of the analytic interaction.

The inclusion of countertransference response in determining whether a patient is treatable—that is, treatable with a particular analyst—is no longer based

---

Much of the professional literature is directed toward questions that stress how we perceive and react toward patients.

---

on the evaluation of the patient alone. In many quarters, this unidimensional approach has been replaced by an examination of the interaction between both participants in the treatment relationship. Analysts examine their personal responses as well as the patient's defensive adaptations, intrapsychic conflicts, and structural defects. Clinicians attempt to predict potential transference projections and then measure their anticipated responses. The questions frequently asked are whether the therapeutic setting can survive taking into account the therapist's vulnerabilities as well as areas of strength and whether it is possible to construct an effective holding environment. This does not mean that the course of treatment is, in fact, predictable, as has been discussed by earlier generations of analysts.

There is, however, an atmosphere, a feeling tone, often evident even in the first interview, that sets the stage for the future analytic interaction. If this initial feeling is positive, the patient eventually forms a bond with the therapist that is in many ways similar to that described by neonatologists. Such a felicitous response may be the outcome of a feeling of comfortable security and even perhaps familiarity, even though the analyst has never seen the patient before and is unaware of the possibility that a stormy analysis lies ahead.

From *Countertransference Triumphs and Catastrophes.* See page 188.

Peter Giovacchini, M.D., is Clinical Professor Emeritus of Psychiatry at the University of Illinois College of Medicine and in the private practice of psychoanalysis in Chicago.

11

Short-Term
Psychotherapy

Gregory P. Bauer and Joseph C. Kobos

In short-term psychodynamic psychotherapy, resistive maneuvers are brought to the patient's attention as they occur. This rapid focus on resistance heightens the level of anxiety within the session. A "fight or flight" syndrome may be stimulated in some patients, especially early in treatment. It is critical that the therapist meticulously attend to the patient's moment-to-moment responses. The patient's reaction to interventions by the therapist provides direct feedback as to the patient's ability to respond to the technique used in short-term therapy. Malan believed that the essential nature of this feedback consists of changes in the level of rapport. The ability to evaluate level of rapport is one of the therapist's most essential tasks. Rapport is the universal indicator by which the therapist may be constantly guided. If rapport increases after an intervention, the intervention was appropriate and appropriately made; if rapport decreases, the intervention was inappropriate (not necessarily wrong), and the therapist must reconsider.

In short-term therapy initial feedback often consists of increased resistance. This most frequently is due to the emphasis placed on confronting patient defenses. In many patients, however, once defenses are challenged, and the underlying feeling reached, the patient experiences relief and hope. To illustrate:

> ET was a 25-year-old woman who sought treatment due to problems in interpersonal relationships. ET was conflicted around the expression of anger. Her inability to deal effectively with negative affect resulted in frustration and repressed anger. These feelings were expressed

in derivative fashion (i.e., sarcasm and cynicism). As the therapist developed a clearer
understanding of this pattern, he brought it to
ET's attention and encouraged its examination.
Although ET became threatened and uncomfortable when her accustomed means of
expressing aggressive feelings was confronted,
she responded with relief when the therapist
was able to help her view a core problem (i.e.,
inability to express angry feelings).

Davanloo observed that the following pattern
occurs repeatedly: (1) the patient's defensive patterns
are challenged, (2) they initially become more rigid,
but (3) when the therapist succeeds in penetrating the

If rapport increases after an intervention, the intervention
was appropriate and appropriately made.

---

defenses, there is increasing rapport. The patient in
one way or another is more in touch with previously
defended-against feelings. The tension then drops within the therapeutic situation. The great majority of
patients respond positively to increased awareness of
repressed feelings, as well as to the therapist's understanding. This is reflected in an increased willingness
to collaborate, that is, an increase in motivation and
therapeutic alliance. Such a response assures the therapist of the correctness of the approach.

   At the other end of the spectrum of responses,
the patient may present evidence of being too fragile

to withstand the impact of uncovering repressed material. Challenging patient defenses and exploring underlying feelings may induce such anxiety that the patient regresses to more primitive coping strategies (e.g., massive denial, projection, withdrawal, impulsive acting out). Careful attention should be given to signs of extreme regression, fluidity of thought processes, and other symptoms of adverse patient reaction that suggest an intolerance of interpersonal and intrapsychic anxiety and a need for more supportive technique.

In general, patients who will have difficulty working in an uncovering treatment are identified during assessment. However, at all times the therapist needs to monitor patient reaction to interventions and evolving material, rapport, and therapeutic alliance. Questions for the therapist to consider may include: (1) Is the patient able to develop and maintain an observing ego and to objectively view what is occurring in therapy (i.e., is the patient able to take a realistic look at conflicted feelings and interactive patterns, even while experiencing threat and anxiety)? (2) Does the therapist feel an empathic connection with the patient? Inability to maintain feelings of "being with" the patient may point to a use of withdrawal and avoidance defenses by the patient. (3) With confrontation, do the patient's defenses become more primitive (e.g., patient gives up intellectualizing and begins to use massive projection or denial)? (4) When defenses are confronted, is the patient able to relinquish them momentarily to further explore himself and relate in a less conflicted manner to the therapist?

The discussion of handling resistance in short-term psychodynamic psychotherapy may convey an impression of the therapist as a gadfly who persistently torments the patient's defenses in an unrelenting fashion, or perhaps a military commander whose goal is to locate, attack, and overcome the defensive outposts of the opposition. In effective treatment the therapist does not attack defenses in an effort to break through, destroy them, and get at repressed feelings. The development of such an adversarial stance severely compromises the therapeutic alliance. It is unempathic, persecuting, and doomed to failure in most cases.

An adversarial stance is unempathic, persecuting,
and doomed to failure in most cases.

Short-term psychotherapy places emphasis on analysis of resistance and defense. This emphasis, however, first takes the form of identifying with the patient's attitudes and behaviors that impede his ability to use therapy and interact effectively with the therapist. Emphasis is then put on identifying the role of these defenses in the patient's life and finally on the purpose of these defenses (i.e., avoidance of underlying feelings). This is a large order in a brief treatment. It requires a patient who can quickly become a partner in this venture and who does not lose heart (i.e., motivation) when coping mechanisms are being questioned. It requires a therapist who is able to quickly identify the patient's defensive strategies and is able to help the patient take a look at them as well.

In short-term therapy the therapist actively focuses attention on patient resistance and attempts to help the patient understand how it is played out in therapy. Such a stance is empathic with the importance a patient's defensive strategies play in psychic functioning. An attempt to knock defenses aside without first studying them with the patient will lead to increasing rigidity as the patient gathers forces to protect against an unempathic assault on the most successful means of coping with problems that the patient has been able to develop.

Studying a patient's methods of coping with threat and anxiety is helpful in enabling a patient to learn new methods of dealing with stress elicited by psychic conflict. Short-term psychodynamic psychotherapy will not eliminate a patient's emotional conflicts, but it can give the patient the experience of effectively working on a number of issues.

From *Brief Therapy: Short Term Psychodynamic Intervention.* See page 188.

Gregory P. Bauer, Ph.D., is Distinguished Psychologist, University of Wisconsin-Stevens Point Counseling Center.

Joseph C. Kobos, Ph.D., is Director of the Counseling Service, Office of Student Services, and Professor, Department of Psychiatry, University of Texas Health Science Center at San Antonio.

> *Good intentions are not enough.*

12

Applying the Principles of Supportive Psychotherapy

Marc H. Hollender and Charles V. Ford

Of all of our therapeutic modalities, supportive psychotherapy is the most widely used and the least uniformly taught. All too often it is assumed that good intentions and everyday intuition are all that is required. Consequently, it is not unusual to tell beginning clinical trainees to provide supportive psychotherapy and then cut them loose with little or no supervision. Although the help that they may provide patients should not be denigrated, there is a difference between being supportive and applying the principles of supportive psychotherapy in a skillful and systematic manner with specific objectives and goals in mind.

Questions raised in discussing supportive psychotherapy include the following: "For whom is this form of treatment indicated?" "What is being supported?"

and "What are the specific techniques employed to provide the desired support?"

Supportive psychotherapy is similar to insight-oriented psychotherapy in that both are built on the therapist's understanding of the patient's psychodynamics. They differ, however, in how that understanding is used. In supportive psychotherapy, the therapist's knowledge of the patient's psychodynamic structure may shape the therapeutic approach but seldom serves as the basis for interpretations.

The goal is to strengthen defenses, restore the previous psychological homeostasis, reduce anxiety, and increase the tolerance for unalterable situations. For acute disorders the objective is likely to be the restoration of an equilibrium, and for chronic disorders bolstering the patient whenever and wherever the need arises. In both situations, the development of a

positive transference is fostered, observed, and used; an effort is made to eliminate a negative transference if it appears.

Supportive psychotherapy is the treatment of choice when external pressures threaten to be overwhelming or when internal resources are severely limited by ego weakness or defect. Advanced age and impaired physical condition frequently favor the use of supportive measures.

The decision to employ supportive techniques as the primary therapeutic strategy must be based, as is the case with all types of psychotherapy, on the findings of the evaluation and an understanding of the psychodynamics involved.

The therapist needs to be relatively active but without crowding the patient.

The evaluation and formulation should take into account (1) the patient's ego strength and weakness, (2) recent losses or other stressors that may have resulted in a reduction of self-esteem, (3) the nature of defense mechanisms and the degree that they may be helpful or harmful in coping with stress, (4) the extent that intoxicating chemicals affect the current level of functioning, and (5) the highest level of functioning previously achieved and the circumstances.

From the evaluation, certain principles evolve that can be employed in treatment planning. Among these are the axiom that the most basic functions must be supported best, for example, reality testing in the psychotic patient or the preservation of life in a despondent, severely depressed patient. It is unlikely that psychotherapy of any type can be effective in the face of ongoing substance abuse and this must be addressed directly. It is also unrealistic to expect patients to reach a higher level of functioning than they had achieved in the past. Therefore, one treatment strategy is to help them reinstitute the life circumstances, including the coping mechanisms, associated with their highest level of previous functioning.

As a general rule, the therapist in this kind of therapy needs to be relatively active but without crowding the patient. Dependency should be accepted to an appreciable extent but kept within workable limits by controlling the frequency and length of sessions and telephone calls. For some patients, setting a definite length of time for therapy in advance may be helpful. The effect of psychotherapy may also be augmented by the use of medication, or treatment may consist primarily of manipulation, direct or indirect, of the patient's environment.

From *Dynamic Psychotherapy: An Introductory Approach.* See page 189.

Marc H. Hollender, M.D., is Professor of Psychiatry Emeritus at Vanderbilt University School of Medicine in Nashville, Tennessee.

Charles V. Ford, M.D., is Professor of Psychiatry at the School of Medicine, University of Alabama at Birmingham.

> *Staying calm, even when confused,*
> *is half the battle.*

13

How Theory Helps the Therapist

Sanford Shapiro

Talking to patients exposes us to enormous pressures to understand what we are hearing, to be helpful, and to avoid being harmful. When we feel inundated by material we do not understand, we frequently become anxious, and our anxiety, if sensed by our patients, could be frightening to them. Staying calm, even when confused, is half the battle; staying emotionally connected with our patients is the other half.

Theory provides a structure that helps us organize our thinking, remain calm, and stay connected. Lindon says we need theories "to help us organize what otherwise is a chaotic jumble of meaningless material and to widen our perceptual scope." Staying con-

Sanford
Shapiro

nected with patients is hard when we doubt ourselves, but having a theory to anchor us, even one
that challenges our own, helps us maintain that connection. It gives us the confidence to assure our
patients that we will get through these difficulties
together, even if we do not understand everything
that is happening.

Although we have learned much about the psychoanalytic process, much that takes place in psychoanalysis is yet to be understood. Therefore, we cannot
take our theories for granted, but must be willing to
question them, aware that while theory can help us, it
can also hinder us. Theory, followed too closely, can
lead to mechanical behavior and can stifle creativity. It
can lull us into a false sense of security when we think
we understand, and then encourage us to jump to con-
clusions and prematurely discontinue necessary psy-

choanalytic investigation. Knowing the next question may be more important than knowing the answer.

Theory, the way we understand clinical material, influences how we talk to patients, and is conveyed to

---

Staying calm, even when confused, is half the battle; staying emotionally connected with our patients is the other half.

---

patients by our attitudes and interpretations. Yet theory does not always translate into technique, and research shows that analysts from the same theoretical school may work very differently, while analysts from differing theoretical schools may work similarly.

From *Talking with Patients: A Self Psychological View.* See page 189.

Sanford Shapiro, M.D., is in the private practice of psychoanalysis in La Jolla, California.

14

Sexual Feelings about the Therapist

Glen O. Gabbard

One sparkling fall day when I was a young psychiatry resident, I walked into my cramped cubicle,
euphemistically referred to as an office, and I sat down
across from my patient. Ms. S, a shy young woman
about my age, stared intently at me and blurted out, "I
think I'm in love with you."

With masterful poise I responded, "What do you
mean?"

Ms. S looked at me incredulously,
"What do I mean?! Just what I said! I
think I'm in love with you. Look, don't
make this any harder than it already is.
My sister's in therapy, and she said I
should tell you."

The already confining dimensions
of my consulting room suddenly

*Glen O.
Gabbard*

seemed even smaller. My throat was dry and the pounding of my heart was palpable in my ears. I contemplated my options carefully. I could, of course, run out of the office screaming (a course of action that seemed most in keeping with my affective state). I could be silent and mysterious in the same way my analyst was with me. I could explain to her that her feelings were a form of resistance to the therapy and tell her to stop having such feelings. I could fake a nosebleed and tell her I'd be right back after tending to it (that would at least buy some time to think).

I leaned back in my chair (trying to get a bit of distance from the patient's intensity), and I tried to look as thoughtful and accepting as I could. In a reassuring way I said to the patient, "Well, this sort of thing happens quite frequently in psychotherapy."

Ms. S glared back at me: "How is that supposed to

help me?"

"Well, uh, it may make you feel a little less embarrassed about it if you know you're not alone with these kinds of feelings."

"Oh, so you mean all the girls you treat fall in love with you? That's supposed to make me feel better? To be one of your harem girls?"

"No, no, you misunderstand me," I explained. "I meant psychotherapy patients in general often experience loving feelings for their therapist. I wasn't talking about my own patients in particular."

"That may be true," Ms. S responded, "but I'm not just any patient. I am really in love with you. This isn't the kind of love a patient has for a therapist. This is real love. You're exactly the kind of man I've been looking for."

My patient Ms. S, a shy young woman about my age, stared intently at me and blurted out, "I think I'm in love with you."

At this point in the session, I had an ominous feeling that Ms. S wasn't going to be easy to reason with on this matter and that I wasn't going to be able to extricate myself from the situation with my dignity intact. I assumed a bit of a didactic posture and explained, "I hear what you're saying, but I don't think the feelings are as real as you think they are."

"Not real?! Don't tell me these feelings aren't real. I've been in love before. I know what love is. Besides, how would you know whether my feelings are real anyway?"

Undaunted, I continued: "What I mean is that the feelings stem from old relationships in your past. Maybe they're closely related to feelings you had for your father."

The patient guffawed at the suggestion: "My father? That's a good one, Sigmund. My dad was a jerk. I never felt this way towards him." At this point, my thoughts were racing. I was interpreting the erotic transference as a manifestation of oedipal longings for her father, just like I was taught, but it just wasn't working.

Ms. S continued to rail at me: "What am I supposed to do with these feelings? You're the therapist! I know we can't go out together, but I'm still stuck with these feelings."

---

*Much of my struggle with Ms. S was related
to my own feelings about her and uncertainty
about the way to handle them.*

Like many patients in therapy with supervised trainees, Ms. S was not to receive an answer to the question until a week later, after I'd had the opportunity to speak with my supervisor. I met with him two days later and recounted what had happened. He irritated me no end by repeatedly chuckling to himself as I read from my notes and described my struggles. At one point he noted, "It sounds like she tickled your balls a little?

"Come again?" I replied.

"I think she's exciting you," he clarified.

"You mean sexually," I queried.

"That's the general idea," he responded.

I reflected a moment and said, "I think I was too flustered to feel any sexual excitement." I paused. My supervisor said nothing. "She is very attractive," I acknowledged. He said, "I think that's the starting point for this discussion."

My supervisor, in his crude but well-meaning way, was trying to help me see that much of my struggle with Ms. S was related to my own feelings about her and uncertainty about the way to handle them, even though my presentation to him had focused on how I should manage her feelings.

Is the love experienced by patient and/or analyst "real"? How does the analyst respond to a patient who professes love? How much of the love is "really" for the analyst, and how much is displaced from other figures

---

Love and hate coexist in the analytic situation.

---

in the patient's past? How does one "help" the patient who is in the throes of transference love? What does it mean to conceptualize love as "resistance" to the analytic work? To what extend does the analyst's "love" for the patient play a role?

The questions raised by my encounter with Ms. S did not confine themselves to the affect of love. One of the most disconcerting aspects about the session described was my sense that Ms. S was growing increasingly angry and hostile towards me the more I tried to clarify and help her deal with her feelings. Indeed, I had the impression that her love was about to be transformed into hate at any moment if I continued to pursue the course I had started. I also can reconstruct the session well enough now, some twenty years later, to know that my supervisor was only partly right. I did find the patient sexually attractive, but that was only half the picture. I also found myself hating her and wanting to escape because of what she was doing to me.

The fact that love and hate coexist in the analytic situation should come as no surprise. One might even say that the two conflicting feelings are inherent in the treatment. Now as a supervisor of and consultant to other analysts, I find myself continuing to ponder some of the same questions that had their seeds on that autumn day long ago in the company of Ms. S.

From *Love and Hate in the Analytic Setting.* See page 190.

Glen O. Gabbard, M.D., is Professor of Psychoanalysis and Education in the Karl Menninger School of Psychiatry and Mental Health Sciences at the Menninger Clinic in Topeka, Kansas.

15

The Psychotherapist as Healer

T. Byram Karasu

An overview of the vast variety of psychotherapies of the last century reveals their attempts to resolve the individual's past and present conflicts and remedy his or her deficits by three major change agents: cognitive mastery, affective experience, and behavioral modification. Yet even when this entire armamentarium is applied, psychological conflicts are relatively resolved, deficits filled, and defects corrected, ultimately patients still experience posttherapeutic dysphoria, a loss of meaning or sense of emptiness, a nonluminous hollow.

There is no structured school of the art of healing—it frames other therapies, but is itself frameless. The healer status is bestowed upon the individual

T. Byram
Karasu

73

by his or her society. Professional degrees for the practice of psychotherapy, including their credentialing
and academic requirements, are forms of social sanc-
tion. However, too much attention is often paid to the
professional training of therapists and not enough to
their personal formation.

The formation of the therapist as healer encompasses personal growth, a broad education that goes
beyond psychotherapy per se, and a life philosophy. It
is for the therapist—as it is for everyone else—the
issue of being and becoming, insofar as the therapist
can help a patient grow only as much as he himself has
grown. That is why what really matters is not schools
of therapy, but the psychotherapists themselves.
Although one's theory is generally reflected in the particular modality he or she chooses to practice, the
"person" of the therapist overrides both the theory

and the school to which one is attached. In fact, therapists' technical skills are contextually tailored manifestations of their personality, although the therapist's self can be in danger of getting lost in the quagmire of polarized theories and allegiances.

Those therapists who become overcommitted to the sciences of psychology, biology, or sociology invariably end up underplaying man's ethical and spiritual dimensions. Other therapists, by overemphasizing specific techniques, whether analyzed or behaviorally manipulated, also make man impersonalized, compartmentalized, calculated (and most recently, "managed"), thereby diminished. The contemporary therapist needs to regain his innocence by not being too scientific or too regimented about people, love, and pathology. He must maintain a certain free margin, an openness, credulity, and even ignorance.

That is why what really matters is not schools of therapy,
but the psychotherapists themselves.

The healer is someone who identifies past and present conflicts and deficits, not in order to resolve, but to transcend them. He accepts the person with all his limitations at the same time as he does not settle for that as an end in itself. Moreover, the healer doesn't just apply various techniques toward the resigned acceptance of human dilemmas, but helps the person toward harmonious emancipation from them.

The healer doesn't treat an illness, or try to cure a person who has an ailment; instead he remains with a person who is in the process of becoming. The healer is not a religious counselor. By contrast, the healer rejects strict formality and substitutes flexibility and freedom.

The healer is not like an analyst. Analysis is founded on the model of sickness. By contrast, the healer believes in a model of health, which is normative and transcends (if not eliminates) diagnoses. He knows that puzzlement is a necessary state that precedes enlightenment.

The healer is not like academic psychotherapists. He doesn't follow standardized procedures in operational manuals that homogenize all treatment. Rather, the approach used is highly improvisational and fully accepts (if not promotes) heterogeneity.

In the consolidation of a soulful and spiritual existence, the therapist continues to come closer to an authentic self.

Healers do not practice New Age therapy. New Age psychotherapies promote search for the self—but never get beyond it. In contrast, the healer seeks the self beyond itself, in order not to be self-preoccupied; in short, he is egoless.

The healer seeks innocence and harmony, cultivates an inner and outer stillness, and partakes of unclassified wonderings. In the consolidation of a soulful and spiritual existence, the therapist continues to come closer to an authentic self. Only such authenticity contains really meaningful therapeutic tools, because what endures ultimately emanates from within.

Finally, alas, the therapist must recognize that this is not a field for spectacular successes (if any field is); as Freud early warned us, every therapy is a relative failure. The tranquillity of the therapist largely depends on the ability to live with optimum disillusionment and still maintain profound faith in all persons, with all their vulnerabilities and strengths. Then healing becomes not so much a profession as a way of being in a harmonious relationship to man and infinite nature, a unified quality of mind and heart and soul.

From *The Psychotherapist as Healer.* See page 190.

T. Byram Karasu, M.D., is presently Professor of Psychiatry at Albert Einstein College of Medicine. He is the editor or co-editor of nine books and the author or co-author of more than 100 papers.

> *Achievements in therapy*
> *bring termination in sight.*

16

The Beginning
of the End

Salman Akhtar

The end of the therapeutic process begins to be in sight with the occurrence of certain structural achievements. At the minimum, such changes include (1) a newly developed or enhanced capacity for experiencing and tolerating ambivalence; (2) a greater ability to empathize with others and the resultant deepening of object relations; (3) the emergence of a more realistic view of oneself; (4) a working through and renunciation of the "someday" and revenge fantasies, at least in their more intense and literal forms; (5) a strengthening of ego as evidenced by better impulse control, greater anxiety tolerance, and enhanced sublimatory tendencies; (6) a diminution of reliance on magical acts or fantasies and alco-

Salman
Akhtar

hol or drugs to control anxiety; (7) a greater capacity for peaceful aloneness; and (8) the gradual replacement of intense, predominantly preoedipal transferences by relatively subtle, oedipal transferences. These developments, however, only herald the beginning of the end, not the end itself. The increasing evidence of these capacities, both within the patient–therapist dyad and in the patient's outside life, is tantamount to the first flickering of the proverbial light at the end of the tunnel.

The process has emotional and cognitive reverberations in both the patient and the therapist. From the patient's perspective, there is (1) a greater trust in the therapist; (2) a true fondest for him—still based on idealization but now including an awareness of the therapist's occasional failures and his more sustained quirks and limitations; (3) a marked

diminution or removal of presenting symptoms; (4) a deeper capacity for, and interest in, the process of understanding his own self, resulting from an identification with the analyzing functions of the therapist; this is akin to what Giovacchini called the formation of an "analytic introject"; (5) a diminution in the felt need of the therapist, a development often accompanied by some anxiety and regressive movements to cling to the therapist; (6) a deeper, more complex view of the patient's parents and a changed relationship with them; and (7) a pleasurable increase in the range of both work- and leisure-related activities.

These structural changes in the patient affect the overall ambience of the treatment hours. Cold silence, pouting withdrawal, hungry pleading, desperate clinging, and sulking bitterness gradually give way to nervous giggling, shy withholding, counterphobic cocki-

ness, sensual teasing, and jealous competitiveness. There is more verbalization and less enactment, more collaboration and less negativism. Parallel to these developments in the patient are those in the therapist. He too begins to feel somewhat relaxed, finding himself freer from the countertransference pull toward taking or avoiding this or that stance.

The process has emotional and
cognitive reverberations
in both the patient and the therapist.

Yet another development is a dawning awareness on the part of both parties that time is passing. The patient begins to mention various life goals more frequently, and the therapist too, often for the first time, becomes aware of time's passage.

From *Broken Structures: Severe Personality Disorders and Their Treatment.* See page 190.

Salman Akhtar, M.D., is Professor of Psychiatry at Jefferson Medical College, and Training and Supervising Analyst at the Philadelphia Psychoanalytic Institute.

17

The Limitations
of Managed Care

Muriel Prince Warren

The language of psychotherapy changed when therapists contracted with insurance companies and became "service providers." The treatment process was once regarded as the "talking cure" in which the patient engaged in a frank and open dialogue with a therapist who intervened with interpretations and clarifying questions. In this process most patients gained a greater understanding of themselves and insights into problems and their causes. They felt better, and often the problem that brought them into therapy was dissipated or reduced to tolerable levels. Although the process worked over time, it was perceived by insurers to be too lengthy and too expensive. Managed care com-

Muriel Prince
Warren

panies found it more expeditious to cover measurable, short-term behavioral change rather than long-term structural change in the patient's psyche.

Managed care's overnight rise to dominance brought with it more than just behavioral management. A fundamental concern with cost-effectiveness led logically to the basic business techniques of project management: establishing long-term goals, choosing short-term tasks or objectives to get there, and tracking the progress from start to finish. Suddenly these issues were incorporated into the mental health lexicon, and psychoanalysis was considered archaic. Gone were the concepts of working through the resistance, repetition compulsion, maintaining a holding environment, and exploring the underlying transference. Even establishing a therapeutic alliance was considered suspect. Free association, a standard treat-

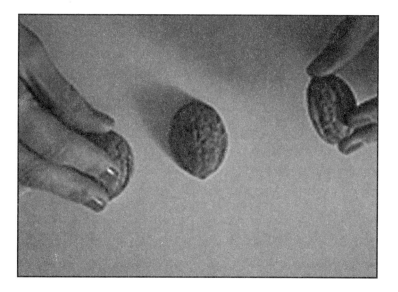

ment mode since the early days of Freud, was replaced by a more focused interaction that could be charted step by step along a predetermined path to the final achievement of its treatment goal.

---

*A fundamental concern with cost-effectiveness
led logically to the basic business techniques
of project management.*

Psychotherapists, who spent years studying the giants of psychiatry and mastering the proven techniques of listening and intervening, suddenly discovered they could not talk to managed care case managers in terms they understood. The language of psychotherapy had changed as the concept of mental disorders gave way to behavioral impairment.

Managed care is concerned with Axis I impair-

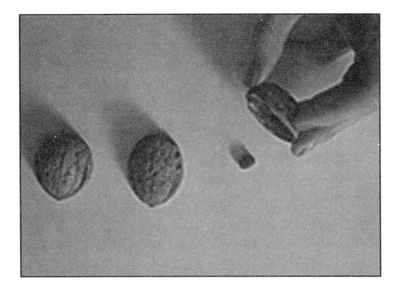

ments. (In *DSM-IV* nomenclature, Axis I refers to clinical disorders that may be a focus of attention, with the exception of personality disorders, which are considered to be Axis II.) If you have a client with an Axis II personality disorder, it becomes a red flag warning of potential long-term treatment that managed care is not prepared to pay for. Insurers do not want to pay for treatment of irresolvable diagnoses, and Axis II diagnoses are usually considered irresolvable. Managed care is also concerned with therapists treating a client for one long-term disorder and transforming him/her over time into a dependent personality disorder. So, if case managers spot a provider with a cluster of long-term clients, they are more apt to refer future clients to other providers who favor short-term treatment.

Insurers are interested in quick, cost-effective change using modalities that are consistent with the client's needs.

Insurers are interested in quick, cost-effective change using modalities that are consistent with the client's needs. Acceptable treatment modalities include cognitive, behavioral, interpersonal, brief dynamic, supportive, group, psychopharmacology, psychological testing, biofeedback, and, depending on the insurance company, hypnosis, sometimes referred to as relaxation techniques. However, it is mostly a matter of semantics, and as a provider you need to be sensitive to the particular buzz words of individual companies.

Treatment frequency is usually crisis-driven. Once a

week is standard, and may temporarily be increased to twice a week. Some companies also may reduce sessions to every other week or once a month as a prelude to termination. Prior approvals are normally required for evaluation of medication by a psychiatrist or for psychological testing.

Medical necessity is the criterion used by managed care companies to authorize sessions. There are various definitions of medical necessity in use today. The term and its meaning are usually published in the insurance companies' provider manuals. It is important to remember that medical necessity is usually limited to resolvable issues. The term resolvable is vague and subject to definition by the insurance company's case manager. In order to cooperate with the patient's insurance reimbursement, clinicians need to learn the language of the payors.

From *Behavioral Management Guide: Essential Treatment Strategies for Adult Psychotherapy.* See page 191.

Muriel Prince Warren, D.S.W., A.C.S.W., is a psychotherapist, author, and educator. She is engaged in private practice in New York City and Rockland County, New York. Dr. Warren is the Executive Director of the Psychoanalytic Center for Communicative Education as well as a senior training and supervising analyst there.

18

Practicing Defensively

Lawrence E. Hedges

1. *The escalation of lawsuit*s in our litigious society places therapists in an increasingly dangerous position.

2. *The demands of accountability* from the public put us in potential jeopardy with state licensing boards and ethics committees.

3. *Our malpractice "deep pocket"* makes us a ready target for clients and attorneys.

4. *The whereabouts of dangerous and potentially litigious people* has changed in modern society. Once locked away in insane asylums and mental hospitals, often tortured as evil or burned at the stake as witches, these badly damaged and often vengeful and dangerous people are now

Lawrence E. Hedges

87

attracted to our psychotherapy consulting rooms.

5. *Tranquilizers and antipsychotic and antidepressant medications* often mask patients' deep relational traumas, giving us the illusion of meaningfully tapping into the developmental sources of their damage. We can be easily deluded by what can be called "archetypal content," "false-self" conformity, "mimical-self" imitation, and "cures" based on transference or resistance.

6. *The expansion of depth-therapy tools* over the past three decades gives us the illusion of omnipotence. Originally invented for the treatment of neurosis in well-developed individuals, psychotherapy theory and practice have now been expanded to include narcissistic, borderline, and organizing (psychotic) levels of development—erroneously leading us to believe that all psychological states are treatable.

7. *Narcissistic, borderline, and organizing "pockets"
exist in all people.* These pockets come in small,
medium, and large! But the most likely to deceive us
are the very small, hidden pockets of madness that
are essentially universal, and the very large multi-
symptomatic pockets that are highly elusive and for-
ever changing in their forms.

8. *We have absolutely no way of determining at the
outset* who in our practice has experienced what
kinds of infantile trauma or neglect, or of knowing
how long-internalized patterns of deprivation, fear,
rage, shame, hatred, and revenge are likely to be reex-
perienced in the transference–countertransference
matrix, or in what ways the therapist may come to be
fused and confused in transference with the original

---

*Experience teaches us that the clients therapists like the best,
are the most invested in, and have done the most for are the
most likely to file complaints and bring lawsuits.*

---

perpetrator of infantile trauma during moments of crisis or extreme stress, or what kinds of accidental or
fluke events in or out of the therapeutic situation may
trigger a dangerous or lethal transference reaction.
Thus, thinking "This person would never sue me" or
"It can't happen to me" is the kiss of death for psychotherapists. Never believe either slogan! Experience
teaches us that the clients therapists like the best, are
the most invested in, and have done the most for are
the most likely to file complaints and bring lawsuits.

9. *Don't be a fool!* As a therapist you treat many deeply
traumatized and damaged people. No matter how

intelligent or emotionally intact the client seems or is, and no matter how much you like or respect the client who comes for help, deep and destructive pockets of psychotic terror and rage may later be unexpectedly opened and aimed at you. You invited the client into your consulting room and encouraged her or him to speak freely. It is then only a matter of time before long-frozen and unmetabolized deep pockets of trauma become activated for reexperiencing in the here-and-now memories of transference and resistance.

10. *Face the challenge: Practice defensively.* You drive your car defensively, you manage your finances defensively, you run your personal life defensively, you must also run your psychotherapy practice defensively! Don't put yourself, your clients, your colleagues, your family, or your personal estate in harm's way by being thoughtless or otherwise careless in your psychotherapy business!

From *Facing the Challenge of Liability in Psychotherapy: Practicing Defensively.* See page 191.

Lawrence E. Hedges, Ph.D., is a psychologist and psychoanalyst in private practice in Orange, California. Dr. Hedges holds Diplomates from The American Board of Professional Psychology and The American Board of Forensic Psychology and is the author of numerous papers and books on the practice of psychoanalytic psychotherapy.

II
Special
Situations

*How adult children of the borderline mother
can develop a reality-based relationship.*

19

Surviving the Borderline Mother

Christine Ann Lawson

Only adult children have the power and freedom necessary to develop a reality-based relationship with their mother. Letting go of unconscious, conditioned reactions, however, requires awareness, practice, and patience. Children of the **Waif** borderline mother who are competent successful adults are often astounded by how easily their mother can shake their self-confidence.

Like a butterfly caught in strong winds, the Waif feels powerless to choose direction or focus. In social situations she flits about, never connecting in depth. She can be inappropriately open, enticing others by too much self-disclosure, and then walking away with an air of indifference. She

*Christine Ann
Lawson*

93

may fish for compliments and then reject them, seek attention and then hide, complain miserably and then refuse help.

The Waif mother's repeated crises, anxious pleadings, medical emergencies, frequent accidents, and financial distresses create anxiety in her adult children. Rescuing behavior perpetuates the Waif's unhealthy emotional dependency because it reinforces her view of herself as helpless.

Adult children must accept responsibility for the way they communicate their needs and feelings. What works for one child may not work for another. Although the Waif behaves unpredictably, adult children can respond in a predictable, consistent manner. The Waif is not helpless. Regardless of the crisis, adult children must give the Waif mother the message that she can and must help herself.

Michelle's mother frequently complained about her finances, her health, and her loneliness. Michelle learned to ask what her mother actually needed, and responded to complaints by clarifying her mother's expectations of her. She would say, "Mother, are you asking me to lend you some money?" or "Are you wanting me to keep you company?" Depending on her mother's response, Michelle explained whether or not she felt capable of meeting her expectations. Adult children need to be consistently direct with the Waif mother.

The **Hermit** borderline mother teaches her children that the world is a dangerous place, because, for her, it was. Unfortunately, the Hermit's adult children need to be cautious about sharing their fears with their mother. Her response most likely will exacerbate their fear and undermine their self-confidence.

The Hermit cannot provide emotional support or bolster her child's self-confidence because she lacks self-confidence herself.

Sandy made the mistake of telling her mother about a conflict with her boss. Her mother catastrophized the situation, telephoning her several times a day, vilifying her boss, suggesting he was "out to get Sandy," implying that Sandy would soon be fired. Sandy found herself having to reassure her mother that she would not be fired, and regretted having told her about the minor disagreement.

The Hermit cannot provide emotional support or bolster her child's self-confidence because she lacks self-confidence herself. Unless someone helps her distinguish between legitimate anxiety and irrational fear, the Hermit's panic can escalate. Sandy said, "Mother, telling me that my boss is out to get me doesn't make me feel better. In fact, it makes me feel worse. When I told you that my boss and I had an argument, I needed you to tell me that you understood my feelings. I am not afraid of being fired for disagreeing with my boss." The Hermit's adult children must separate their fears from their mother's fears.

The **Queen** borderline mother's demands can exhaust her adult children, whom she may view as selfish and disloyal. The Queen's adult children cannot fill their mother's insatiable need for attention or admiration. They cannot compensate for what she did not

---

When adult children place their mother's needs
before their own needs, they not only sacrifice themselves,
but may be sacrificing their marriage.

---

receive as a child. They cannot please her, control her, or change her. They can, however, change how they respond to her. When adult children place their mother's needs before their own needs, they not only sacrifice themselves, but may be sacrificing their marriage.

Ellen and her husband frequently argued about her mother's unreasonable demands. Her husband nicknamed her mother "Queen Anne" because no one dared confront her. Adult children must allow the Queen to rule her life, not theirs. Ellen felt caught in her mother's web of control. When she and her husband were first married, her mother offered to buy them a house. After Ellen discovered that her mother intended to move in with them, she declined the offer. The Queen can lure her children into traps that are built for two.

Like a snake, the **Witch** borderline mother strikes when she is confronted or cornered. The Witch within the Queen may emerge when she feels controlled, or when others fail to admire her or treat her as special. The Witch within the Hermit may appear when she feels invaded, challenged, rejected, or cornered. The Witch within the Waif may appear when she feels blamed, criticized, rejected, or abandoned. Unfortunately, children have little control over when, where, or why the Witch appears. The key to survival lies in escaping her control.

The Witch within the Queen may emerge
when she feels controlled, or when others fail
to admire her or treat her as special.

Power possessed by adult children threatens the Witch's control. An attractive young patient had plunged into despair following a conversation with her mother, who had called her a slut. During the session, a smile emerged through her tears as she discounted the ludicrous charge. Yet she could not shake off the feeling of being soiled. "I feel like I'm 4 years old again, when my mother said she'd be better off without me," she explained. This talented young woman, a caring mother with two young children, was an accountant. The more successful she became, however, the more her mother needed to degrade her.

Rather than retaliate, the patient decided to take a short trip to visit a friend. She reminded herself how grateful she is to be grown up and to have the power to get away from denigration. The single greatest power adult children possess is their ability to get away.

From *Understanding the Borderline Mother: Helping Her Children Transcend the Intense, Unpredictable, and Volatile Relationship.* See page 192.

Christine Ann Lawson, Ph.D., is a clinical social worker in private practice in Indianapolis, Indiana. She has previously served as adjunct faculty at Indiana University-Purdue University, Indianapolis, and Butler University.

20

Psychotherapy with Patients Who Self-Injure

Robin E. Connors

People who directly injure their bodies by cutting, burning, or head banging, for example, are increasingly requesting help from psychotherapists and other health care providers. For many self-injurers, the disclosure of such generally private behavior is fraught with intensity and meaning. As clinicians, we may not initially realize all of what people bring to us when they ask for assistance. For the most part, people who self-injure harbor a deep desire for clinicians to perceive the pain and need beneath their behavior. They long to be understood, respected, and helped in ways that can be difficult to articulate. They seek a listener skilled at hearing the layers of meaning and truth they endeavor to

*Robin E.
Connors*

99

tell through word and action. And they fear, often with good reason, that others will react in a controlling, shaming, or dismissive fashion.

The psychotherapy process with clients who self-injure generally encompasses a wide range of issues and tasks. The self-injury is frequently not the presenting concern, and the client and therapist may determine specific goals for their work together that do not address the self-injury directly in any way. Managed care limitations or other insurance constraints may dictate that the work focus on decidedly concrete and measurable goals, further removing any focus on the self-injury. On the other hand, the self-injury may be identified as the pressing problem. Occasionally it is so named by the client; more often, others in the client's life, such as family members or a mental health professional, have focused their concern on

the self-injuring behavior.

Regardless of the relative importance given to the self-injury at the time of initial contact with the therapist or at the time of disclosure, the task facing the psychotherapist is to work with the client to establish therapeutic goals that meet the client's needs. These may or may not focus on the self-injury itself. Over the course of their work together, they may shine a spotlight on issues related to the self-injuring behavior from time to time, and then refocus on other issues. Rarely is it useful to concentrate solely on the self-injury. If a client struggles with self-injury, a host of other issues also clamor for attention, and to focus solely on self-injury does the client a disservice.

The task facing the psychotherapist is to work with the client to establish therapeutic goals that meet the client's needs. These may or may not focus on the self-injury itself.

Underlying this flexible approach to treatment planning, however, three therapeutic goals regarding a client's self-injury can be conceptualized. The first and most important goal is to encourage communication about self-injury as a relevant aspect of the client's life that has some relationship to his past and other issues of concern. Working consistently to achieve this goal allows the client to address the second and third goals when they are salient for the client. The second goal is to improve the quality of the client's life as it relates to self-injury. This might include reducing shame and isolation, receiving adequate medical attention to the self-injury when needed, and decreasing self-criticism for injuring. The third goal is to significantly diminish the use of self-injury as a coping skill.

The phrase "when they are salient for the client" in the preceding paragraph is a key element in approaching goal-setting about self-injury in the therapy process. Mental health professionals, particularly when pressured to produce measurable outcomes or when uncomfortable with their own reactions to the self-injury, tend to leap to the third goal (diminishing the use of self-injury), either ignoring the first two or simply using them as stepping stones to the third. While the role of nonblaming, affirming communication about a client's experience of self-injury does indeed facilitate the approach to both improving the quality of the client's life in the context of self-injury and potentially reducing the occurrence of self-injury, working toward these latter goals needs to be the client's agenda. Only when the client desires to make changes regarding her behavior about self-injury should the second and third goals become central or even relevant to the therapy process.

From *Self-Injury: Psychotherapy with People Who Engage in Self-Inflicted Violence.* See page 192.

Robin E. Connors, Ph.D., is a clinician and consultant in private practice in Pittsburgh, Pennsylvania.

21

Creating Meaning
Out of Loss

Joanne T. Jozefowski

My work follows the experiences of the courageous people I call the Phoenix Grievers, named after the mythological bird who, after being consumed in flames, rose from the ashes renewed and in a better form. So it is with these unique human beings. They demonstrate the courage and determination that result in a renaissance of body, mind, and spirit in the aftermath of tragedies.

When I started working in the bereavement field, grief theories were dominated by messages such as "survive grief," "get through grief," or, "you'll get through it, but you'll never be the same." Such descriptions imply negative or neutral outcomes and do little to encourage

*Joanne T.
Jozefowski*

grievers to work through the developmental tasks of the process. Only recently are clinicians and theoreticians examining the resiliency of individuals enduring adversity. While indeed a person may not be the same after the death of a loved one, diminishment of self and of life are not the only possible outcomes.

As time went on, I discovered that there are those who can alchemize their pain and despair into something transformative, even inspirational. I came to see that resilience and courage can lead to growth and maturation. And I could not help wondering what makes some grievers surface more empowered than ever, more mature, more compassionate, stronger, while some of the seemingly invulnerable collapse.

None of those I call the Phoenix Grievers has asked for this "opportunity" to evolve. Of course all

would gratefully have their loved ones restored to them. Phoenix Grievers do not bypass the grief process. Rather, they experience its phases, accepts its challenges, and find ways to create meaning out of loss, thus honoring the life of their deceased.

> David, a warm, benevolent, and distinguished gentleman, volunteers in an "Alternatives to Violence" program at a maximum-security prison. His work has helped thousands of prisoners. David's daughter, Ruth, was raped and murdered.

> Noella is a successful psychotherapist, mother, and grandmother, whose helpful hands and loving spirit extend to all in need. Noella's husband, Bob, died when she was 28 years old, leaving her with two young children and no formal education.

What makes some grievers surface more empowered than ever, more mature, more compassionate, stronger, while some of the seemingly invulnerable collapse?

As we search for role models to guide us in times of emotional and spiritual darkness, we may find them in the Phoenix Grievers. They are the experts from whom we can learn to:

- understand our familiarity with grief,
- understand the developmental phases of grief,

- use resources and tools to survive and grow through each phase,
- learn what the Phoenix Grievers were like before and after the death of a loved one and how they grew,
- identify the potential for personal growth during grieving,
- understand grief's opportunities to create meaning and honor to a loved one's life and death,
- understand therapeutic metaphor (parable) as a "language" in grief,
- learn a metaphor (parable) for each phase of the grief process.

Ralph, whose son was murdered, offers these suggestions: "First of all remember, if you can make it to the horizon, it [depression] suddenly breaks. Run, don't walk, to any support group that you can find. Do not, I emphasize this, withdraw into yourself. Find others who can share your experience and understand what it is to go through. Yell, scream, cry, swear, anything to get it out. Don't apologize for this. Ask God, 'What the hell are you doing?' Do not make a habit of taking anything that will alleviate your pain. Go straight for it and straight into it. This is the way to heal.

"I have found that helping others helped me. I walked with them. It taught me patience and tolerance and I learned how to give a person the benefit of the doubt before I passed judgment. I believe it is a sincere privilege to have had the trust of others placed in me."

Many Phoenix Grievers have found comfort and healing through helping others in their struggles with grief. This is one of the strongest threads that these exceptional mourners have in common.

From *The Phoenix Phenomenon: Rising from the Ashes of Grief.* See page 193.

Joanne T. Jozefowski, Ph.D., C.S., is a psychotherapist who specializes in bereavement therapy. She is the founder of Counseling Affiliates, a group practice focusing on issues of loss and grief.

22

Overcoming Relentless Hope

Martha Stark

By way of illustrating the defense of relentless hope, I offer the case of Lin, a young woman who presented recently to treatment with a chief complaint of concern about her husband's insensitivity to her needs and, more generally, his lack of emotional availability. As her story has unfolded, it has become clear that Lin is looking to her husband to be the good mother she never had and, to the extent that he does not do this, she is in an absolute rage at him.

Lin's mother was an extremely narcissistic woman who was relatively impervious to her daughter's needs; in fact, she insisted that her daughter accommodate to her own (the mother's) needs. Lin was never able to feel

*Martha
Stark*

that she really mattered to her mother and was instead left with the feeling that she was invisible. Throughout her life, it has been extraordinarily important to Lin to be able to feel that the important people in her world are able to hold her in their mind, even when she is elsewhere.

As it happens, her husband, Paul, is a very decent man who loves his wife deeply and is devoted to her. Instead of telling her how much he loves her, however, he shows her—in a million little ways and many big ways as well. He wants very much to make her happy and tries hard to accommodate himself to her needs as best he can.

But, over the years, Lin has found herself feeling increasingly frustrated by Paul's "withholding" of verbal expressions of his caring for her. It makes her so angry whenever he forgets to ask her how she is

feeling, or does not think to draw her out, or does not remember from one conversation to the next the issues with which she is most concerned. Furthermore, Lin becomes very upset when Paul is not attuned to her internal state and is not able to intuit exactly what she wants.

Although Paul demonstrates his love for her and his commitment to her by way of doing all kinds of things for her, admittedly he is not as adept at being empathically attuned and emotionally responsive to her. Each time he lets pass an opportunity to make up to her for what she never had as a child, Lin finds herself feeling devastated and therefore redoubles her efforts to extract from him the love she feels she must have.

Eventually, Lin must be able to confront the intolerably painful reality that her objects are never going to be exactly who she would have wanted them to be.

The evidence would suggest that even though Paul is many things, he will never be the kind of man who will be able to talk about feelings or to engage in deep conversation. Nonetheless, Lin continues to hope, hoping against hope, that Paul will eventually become someone who will be able to "talk deeply."

Over time, in the face of Paul's "refusal" to change, Lin has become increasingly outraged, dissatisfied, and resentful. She feels that she cannot live with Paul unless he can be available to her in the ways that she needs him to be; she feels entitled to such availability and tells herself (and him) that it is not unreasonable for her to be expecting this of him.

Lin's relentless efforts to persuade Paul that he ought to be someone he is not are fueled by her refusal to accept that he is, basically, the way he is. Unable to recognize the part she plays by way of her unrelenting desire, Lin holds fast to her conviction that the problem lies within him and derives from his unwillingness to relent.

As long as Lin clings to her desperate desire to have her love objects provide for her in the ways that her mother should have provided for her but did not, then she will be consigning herself to a lifetime of frustration, disappointment, and anger. Eventually, if Lin is ever to get better, she must be able to confront the intolerably painful reality that her objects (whether her husband, her therapist, or the other people in her world) are never going to be exactly who she would have wanted them to be.

In the transference, it will be the therapist's inevitable failures (re-creating for Lin her mother's early-on failure of her) that will offer Lin the opportunity to achieve belated mastery of her heartbreak. When the therapist begins to fail her as her mother once failed her, all the old pain, all the old hurt, will be revived.

But within the context of her relationship with a therapist who understands how devastated she feels and has the capacity to see her through it, Lin will have the opportunity to do now what she could not possibly do as a child. In other words, Lin will be able to confront the reality of just how limited her mother really was and to feel whatever she needs to feel so that she can move on—sadder, perhaps, but no longer consumed by the relentlessness of her infantile desire.

Once the patient has made her peace
with the fact that reality is as it is,
then she will be able to let go of her relentless hope.

It will be by way of grieving that Lin will eventually be able to let go of her illusions and of her entitlement. As Lin confronts the pain of her heartache, she will gradually replace her illusion that her love objects must be for her the good mother she never had with a reality—namely, that she will have to become for herself that good mother. Her need for illusion and her entitlement will be replaced by a capacity to experience and to accept reality as it is.

More generally, although the patient's contention may be that her pain will not go away until her needs have been gratified, my belief is that the patient's pain will not go away until her need for good mothering has been frustrated (optimally frustrated) against a backdrop of gratification.

In other words, the patient must have the experience of working through her optimal disillusionment, of working through the devastation and the outrage that she feels as she begins to confront, head-on, her object's limitations (whether the object is her parent, her therapist, or a significant other). The patient must grieve such limitations and master them.

Ultimately, the patient must move beyond the need to have reality be a certain way, having transformed such a need into the capacity to know and to accept reality as it is, the hallmark of mental health. Once the patient has made her peace with the fact that reality is as it is, then she will be able to let go of her relentless hope and to move on to a deeper and a richer enjoyment of her life and of her relationships.

From *Modes of Therapeutic Action: Enhancement of Knowledge, Provision of Experience, and Engagement in Relationship.* See page 193.

Martha Stark, M.D., a graduate of the Harvard Medical School and the Boston Psychoanalytic Institute, is a Clinical Instructor in Psychiatry at the Harvard Medical School and in private practice in Newton Centre, Massachusetts. Dr. Stark is on the faculty of both the Boston Psychoanalytic Institute and the Massachusetts Institute for Psychoanalysis.

23

Defining the Therapeutic Task with Narcissistic Patients

Sheldon Bach

Increasing understanding of narcissism has widened our diagnostic net beyond the type of narcissist who presents with haughty grandiosity, a sense of entitlement, and shallow and devalued relationships, which I shall call the overinflated narcissistic type. Now we may also include in this category those patients who show the "other side of the coin" and present with complementary feelings of inferiority and hypersensitivity, boredom and uncertainty, and chronic idealizations followed by disillusionments, which I

Sheldon Bach

shall call the deflated narcissistic type. One tends to think that the overinflated narcissistic type has too much pathological narcissism, whereas the deflated narcissistic type has too little healthy narcissism, but we shall later see that this formulation is somewhat oversimplified and that both types share a common defect of representational constancy.

Those overinflated patients who present with grandiosity and entitlement tend to form a mirroring transference, in which the patient insists that the therapist should reflect or mirror the patient's grandiose wishes; whereas those who present with depletion and inferiority tend to form an idealizing transference, in which the patient insists that the therapist should embody his grandiose wishes. While many narcissistic patients alternate between feelings of grandiosity and inferiority, the literature has tended to emphasize the

grandiose or overinflated patient, sometimes reserving other diagnoses such as regressed oral hysteric, infantile personality, or masochistic character for the type who presents with depletion and inferiority. For a long time the treatment of the narcissistic disorders was embroiled in a lively debate between proponents of conflict and of deficit, but the passage of time suggests that framing the issues in these terms is not entirely clarifying, if only because it now seems apparent that developmental deficits lead to unresolvable conflicts and that unresolvable conflicts engender developmental failures.

Although overinflated and deflated narcissists are ideal types reflecting only presenting aspects of the

---

The therapeutic task is to uncover the sense of depletion in the overinflated narcissist and to uncover the grandiosity in the deflated type.

---

personality, I include both in the diagnosis of narcissism because I feel that the one is often simply the overt or the covert face of the other. Indeed, an important part of the therapeutic task consists in uncovering the sense of depletion and inferiority in the overinflated-type narcissist and in uncovering the grandiosity and entitlement in the deflated-type narcissist. I also include on this continuum certain patients with narcissistic character disorders who present with symptoms of perversion, addiction, eating disorders, or psychosomatic complaints, because I believe these are structurally related and therefore show a similar evolution in the transference and treatment. I might mention here my impression that these patients frequently show a history of unusual sensitivities as young children, so that they might require unusually nurturant or devoted parenting to successfully manage their unusual temperaments.

In all these conditions there appears to be a difficulty with evocative constancy, that is, a weakened capacity to evoke or hold on to the object representation when the object is absent, or to hold on to the self representation when the object is not there to sustain it. The overinflated narcissist is someone whose sense of his objects is fading and who compensates by overinflating himself and insisting he is so powerful that he doesn't need objects, whereas the deflated narcissist is someone whose sense of himself is fading and who compensates by overinflating an object and then clinging to this idealized figure for stability.

From *The Language of Perversion and the Language of Love.* See page 194.

Sheldon Bach is Clinical Professor of Psychology at the New York University Postdoctoral Program in Psychoanalysis and is in private practice in New York City.

24

Working with Borderline Patients

Otto Kernberg

Clinically, when we speak of patients with bor-derline personality organization, we refer to patients who present serious difficulties in their interpersonal relationships and some alteration of their experience of reality but with essential preser-vation of reality testing.

Such patients also present contradictory character traits, chaotic coexistence of defenses against and direct expression of primi-tive "id contents" in consciousness, a kind of pseudo-insight into their per-sonality without real concern for or awareness of the conflictual nature of this material, and a lack of clear identi-ty and lack of understanding in depth of other people. These patients present

*Otto
Kernberg*

primitive defensive operations rather than repression and related defenses, and above all, mutual dissociation of contradictory ego states reflecting what might be called a "nonmetabolized" persistence of early, pathological internalized object relationships. They also show "nonspecific" manifestations of ego weakness. The term "nonspecific" refers to lack of impulse control, lack of anxiety tolerance, lack of sublimatory capacity, and presence of primary process thinking, and indicates that these manifestations of ego weakness represent a general inadequacy of normal ego functions. In contrast, the primitive defensive constellation of these patients and their contradictory, pathological character traits are "specific" manifestations of ego weakness. In short, they represent highly individualized, active compromise formations of impulse and defense.

One has to keep in mind that ego weakness does not reflect absence of a solid defensive organization of the ego, but represents the very active presence of a rigid constellation of primitive defenses; these defenses by their effects contribute to producing and maintaining such ego weakness. Second, rather than attempting to reinforce higher-level defenses or to support the patient's adaptation directly, it is helpful to consistently interpret these primitive defensive operations, especially as they enter the transference, because the interpretation of these defenses permits ego growth to resume and higher-level defensive operations to take over. Third, interpretations have to be formulated so that the patient's distortions of the

---

Interpreting these primitive defensive operations, especially as they enter the transference, permits ego growth to resume.

---

analyst's intervention can be simultaneously and systematically examined, and the patient's distortion of present reality and especially of his perceptions in the hour can be systematically clarified. This clarification does not mean suggestion, advice giving, or revelation regarding personal matters of the analyst to the patient, but a clear explanation of how the analyst sees the "here and now" interaction with the patient in contrast to how the analyst assumes the patient is interpreting this "here and now" interaction. Clarification of perceptions and of the patient's relationship to the interpretation is, therefore, an important component of an essentially interpretive approach which attempts to systematically analyze the primitive defensive constellation as it enters the transference.

From *Borderline Conditions and Pathological Narcissism.* See page 194.

Otto Kernberg, M.D., F.A.P.A., is Associate Chairman and Medical Director of the New York Hospital-Cornell Medical Center, Westchester Division, and Professor of Psychiatry at the Cornell University Medical College.

25

Treatment of Stress Response Syndromes

Mardi Horowitz

Stress response syndromes include emotional flooding with intrusive images and ideas. To avoid dreaded states of mind, people automatically inhibit information processing. That leads to states of denial, numbing, and avoidance. Because of avoidance behavior, attention to defensive coping and resistance to treatment is important. Hence, a cognitive-dynamic approach addresses patterns of defensive coping, as well as efforts to counteract dysfunctional beliefs and disturbances in roles of self and others.

Mardi Horowitz

The goal of treatment is to help the person work through the linkage between self and the stressor events so that all such symptoms can be attenuated or terminated. The aim is to help the patient so he or she is neither blunted nor emotionally flooded, and is restored to a pre-event level of functioning.

The goal of treatment is to help the person work through the linkage between self and the stressor events so that all such symptoms can be attenuated or terminated.

Real evaluation and treatment may be seamless; however a didactic division of it into phases helps indicate how techniques may usefully change over time. In the following case example, these phases will be discussed:

1. Evaluation and formulation (includes diagnosis and formulation, establishing an alliance and plan for treatment).

2. Initial support (At the biological level, this may include prescription of medications, restored nutrition, and more rest. At the social level, supportive measures include time structuring, advising other people who have contact with the patient, and other contextual interventions. At the psychological level, supportive measures involve the establishment of a therapeutic relationship and a plan for treatment.)

3. Exploration of meanings (Once the patient is capable of working states in which intense, unpleasant emotions can be tolerated, the stressor event's meanings to self can be examined.)

4. Improving coping (Attitudes that lead to unnecessary avoidances are interpreted.)

5. Working through (The goal is to help a problem-

atic response to stress come to be like adaptive responses.)

6. Terminating (Working through emotions about separating and reinforcing corrective beliefs and attitudes.)

CASE EXAMPLE:

Frank was a 25-year-old male lifeguard at a neighborhood pool. On one busy summer day, the pool was full of children and adolescents. Besides there being many people in the water, unruly episodes were occurring on the deck. Frank was quite busy and realized that he was so overloaded with demands for his attention that he could not be sure that everyone was safe. Frank blew his whistle and ordered the pool cleared.

To his horror, there was an inert body at the bottom of the pool. He dove in at once and brought a small, limp, non-breathing figure to the deck. Frank began cardiopulmonary resuscitation. This failed to revive the small boy, who was later pronounced dead. Overcome with remorse, Frank went to the funeral of the deceased child. He was greeted with many angry scowls and became upset by the grief-stricken faces of the child's parents.

Frank went through turbulent periods of remorse, insomnia, attacks of anxiety, guilt, shame, and developed a dread of dying. He quit his job, had difficulty concentrating, and avoided pools, children, and the neighborhood where he had worked as a lifeguard.

Six months after the event, Frank began having frightening nightmares, with visual images of a dead body in a pool, a blurred face of a child, and angry faces of adults. He was preoccupied with feelings of remorse, which disrupted his concentration at his new job. He had outbursts of anger with companions. These intrusions occurred despite his efforts to avoid them.

Frank was remote and apathetic when pressed for details about his current feelings. It was hard to clarify those subjects that seemed to cause his most dreaded states. This was ameliorated as the therapist indicated empathic and compassionate recognition of his suffering. Frank was then able to move toward an exploration of the topic that seemed important: he had entangled realistic and fantastic aspects of his responsibility as a lifeguard for the safety of everyone in the pool. He felt terribly guilty; it was necessary to get beyond his surface statements that he had already worked through this issue. He used warding-off rationalizations, saying how "it was the fault of others."

To shed guilt, he externalized blame onto pool managers for putting him in an overly demanding situation. As it happened, exploring this topic led to a negative reaction toward the therapist, including rage that the therapist was expecting too much from him. A warded-off but emergent feeling that "recovery was too good for him" was clarified. Frank brought up a past memory of how he, at age five, had piled toys onto his unwanted two-year-old brother in an effort to get rid of him. This past memory added intensity to his guilt.

Exploring this topic led to a negative reaction toward the therapist, including rage that the therapist was expecting too much from him.

In a phase of improving coping, the plan was to focus on the current stressor. Frank was asked to explore the question of how much remorse he needed to feel in order to reduce his sense of guilt. As Frank worked on this issue, he decided to volunteer his services in teaching drowning prevention to schoolchildren even though it made him tense and anxious. He saw how he could be constructive; this differed from a need to be self-punitive, as in seeking to fail in his current career efforts.

Frank was at an intrusive phase of response with many continuing avoidant responses. In the phase of initial support, the treatment plan was to empathically accept him as suffering and worthy of help, as well as needing a therapeutic process. A phase of exploring meanings was to begin in an initial treatment session. Several topics were designated, and working through phases on these topics would follow.

In the termination phase, the plan was to help Frank feel less dependent on the therapist in order to shore up his sense of identity; he feared relapse after the treatment ended. By the next-to-last session, he felt that he could stop at the appointed time, provided booster visits could be available as needed. This plan was agreed upon.

From *Stress Response Syndromes: Fourth Edition.* See page 195.

Mardi Horowitz, M.D., is Professor of Psychiatry at the University of California, San Francisco.

26

Management of Severe Rejecting Behavior

Jeffrey Seinfeld

This essay is about the clinical management of the borderline patient's severe rejecting behavior in the transference relationship. The patient suffered from extreme environmental hardships. It can be demonstrated that the therapist can respond to the patient to facilitate the internalization of the therapist as a helping object. These interventions are particularly relevant during the out-of-contact and symbiotic phases of the transference evolution. The issue of countertransference is also important.

Jeffrey Seinfeld

Diane

Diane is a 29-year-old Hispanic woman seeking help for her latency-age son, who was having academic and behavioral problems in school. She had also been reported to the child welfare authorities for child abuse and neglect before coming for help. I have been treating Diane for five years.

Diane grew up in a large family supported by public assistance. She and her siblings were severely abused by an embittered mother. Once, after Diane and her mother had quarreled, her mother beat her with a metal rod until she was covered with blood. Such incidents resulted in the temporary removal of Diane and her siblings from the home by child welfare authorities on several occasions. Diane's father, an alcoholic, deserted the family during Diane's childhood.

Diane made a serious suicide attempt in adolescence and left home permanently at the age of 16. She began to live with a man, became pregnant, and left him when he asked her to marry him. She said that she

wanted no part of an emotional commitment.

Since that time, Diane has lived with her son and has worked sporadically at various jobs. She generally sought temporary positions where she could make her own hours and work independently. Unable to get along with supervisors or co-workers, she would quit or get fired. She moved around a great deal and was evicted on occasion for not paying the rent.

---

*The therapist can facilitate the internalization
of the therapist as a helping object.*

The Problem of the Patient Acting
Rather Than Reflecting

Diane began treatment on a once-weekly basis. There was hyperactivity about Diane. She would sit on the edge of her seat, as if she were ready to pounce, shifting about uncomfortably and continually looking at her watch. She did not stay for the full 45-minute session but left after "saying her piece."

Her constant crises were always the focus of our sessions. It felt absurd to focus on our relationship when she had such pressing reality problems, so we would discuss these problems week after week, but nothing ever seemed to change. She would resolve one crisis or problem only to encounter another one. I felt that we were going around in circles, that her reality problems stood between us, and also that she did not have a significant enough internal relationship with me to use my help. I felt that this patient needed an intense transferential experience in order to begin to cope with and change her environmental situation. I decided to begin to address all of these issues with her.

Tracking the Absence of an Internal Object

The point of entry was her habit of missing appointments and disappearing at irregular intervals. I did not approach this problem from the perspective of resistance or limit setting. Rather, I became intrigued with how she experienced, or did not experience, our relationship during these absences. I thought of myself as a professional helping person, and intellectually at least, she accepted this designation of my role. She realized that she was in something called psychotherapy with me, and she came in and discussed problems in the role of a patient. On an emotional level, howev-

er, at least during certain periods, she did not seem to expect any help. I said this to her and added that when she disappeared, she did not have a picture in her head of me as being able to help her. I guessed that she did not expect help at these times.

I became intrigued with how she experienced, or did not experience, our relationship during these absences.

She explained that during times of severe stress, such as when she was unemployed, short of money, or in danger of eviction, "the thought of you does not enter my head. I completely forget that you, that even this office, exists."

I said, "Then you are all alone with the problem."

She replied, "I've been alone all my life. I've always solved my problems alone."

I said, "Sometimes that has worked. But sometimes the problems seem too great for you to handle all by yourself. They seem insurmountable, overwhelming, and since you feel all alone, you feel totally hopeless to manage them, so you give up and become depressed, and in giving up, there is then no chance to change anything."

I asked her what happened to her relationship to me in her mind between our sessions. She looked at me as if I were crazy and said that she never thought of it. I asked whether she ever thought of me or the therapy when she was faced with a problem. When she felt depressed or angry, did she ever reflect on what we had discussed? "Never," she replied.

I said, "It's like I disappear for you when you leave."

She replied, "Yes, and I'm like that with everyone and everything. I forget that my own son exists. People get angry at me because I forget appointments or don't call them. I don't do it on purpose; it just happens. It's always been like that. So you know, I never even thought about it before." Laughing, she added, "It's not normal, is it?"

I replied, "When you forget about everyone in your life, you are always all alone inside."

She replied, "Sometimes I feel very isolated. Not lonely. I don't want other people's company. I like being alone. But sometimes I feel that there is no place for me, like I'm an outcast. I never fit in anywhere. I didn't fit in with my family. I didn't fit in with other kids, and I can't fit in on a job. I always feel misplaced."

Now when she failed to come for appointments, I called her five minutes into the session. I told her that I was doing so in order to help her remember me and our relationship. I would call, and she would say that she had forgotten. Then she would run to the clinic, which was a few blocks from her apartment. She now said, "I'm crazy. Don't feel that you have to say I'm not. I'm not sensitive at all. I've actually known I was crazy, but I never knew exactly how. Now I'm starting to see."

From *The Bad Object: Handling the Negative Therapeutic Reaction in Psychotherapy*. See page 195.

Jeffrey Seinfeld, Ph.D., is Associate Professor at New York University School of Social Work and is in the private practice of psychotherapy in New York City.

27

Psychotherapy with the Schizoid Patient

Philip Manfield

Schizoids are found far less frequently in psychotherapy than they are in the general population because the nature of their condition makes it unlikely that they would attempt to solve their internal problems by entering into a relationship, especially one with the emotional intensity of psychotherapy. On the contrary, the schizoid seeks safety in emotional and interpersonal distance. Change in interpersonal relationships is extremely threatening to schizoid people so they tend to become tenaciously attached to their existing interpersonal relationships, even if these relationships are abusive. When faced with the possibility of rocking the boat with the apparently remote hope of feeling less iso-

Philip Manfield

lated, the schizoid person generally chooses to maintain the adaptation that has been keeping him safe.

The Role of Fantasy

Especially for the lower level schizoid, fantasy serves as his tenuous tether to the world of relatedness. To make the schizoid's isolation tolerable, he maintains an extensive and rich fantasy life in which he is involved in intimate relationships or in which he holds a prominent social position that allows him to be easily related to other people. Because of its vital importance, this fantasy life will remain hidden from others, including the therapist, and may not emerge in all its richness until well into the treatment process. It is a far more prominent feature for the lower level schizoid who finds both object relations units to be intolerable than it is for the higher level schizoid who

can adapt to a master/slave existence.

Case Example—the Role of Fantasy

Mr. M. is an example of a lower level schizoid who relied on fantasy to help him live with his extreme isolation. He was a young man who had few social contacts in his life. He worked, as do many middle to lower level schizoid individuals, at a civil service job where his income was secure, and he was not called upon extensively to relate to other people. He would go to work in the morning and then come home in the evening and remain in his bedroom looking at pornographic photographs of women. The schizoid's fantasy life can often focus on sex, either as a formula for connectedness or as a sadomasochistic projection of the master/slave unit. Mr. M. engaged in these fantasies to the exclusion of meaningful relationships in the real world.

To make the schizoid's isolation tolerable,
he maintains an extensive and rich fantasy life.

He entered treatment shortly after a problem developed at work between him and his direct supervisor. As a result of this conflict he felt that the supervisor was attempting to get rid of him, and he began behaving in a withdrawn way that appeared paranoid and somewhat bizarre to his co-workers. Eventually a human resources worker suggested that he go to an E.A.P. (Employee Assistance Program) counselor who referred him to treatment. His main motivation for pursuing treatment was the fear of losing his job. He hoped in treatment to learn what he could do to appease his supervisor and other people at work and regain a sense of security.

At first his therapist misjudged Mr. M.'s difficulties in relating to others. She suggested to him that he could not overcome his difficulties with people if he continued to hide out at home and avoid people. In the session that followed she was pleased to hear from Mr. M. that he had ventured outside of his home one evening and gone for a walk during which he had been tempted to approach a young woman who was showing interest in him. Encouraged by Mr. M.'s initial responsiveness, the therapist challenged his use of pornography, saying that he was using it defensively to avoid facing the world and improving his life. In response to these comments, Mr. M. responded initial-

---

The patient's main motivation for pursuing treatment was the fear of losing his job.

---

ly with the compliance of the master/slave unit. His temptation to approach the woman he had seen during his walk was probably no more than a fantasy he had nurtured about approaching the woman. When the therapist challenged his use of pornography to embellish his fantasies, Mr. M. felt misunderstood and attacked. His response was to go into exile, canceling his next two sessions. In general, the schizoid's use of fantasy, although defensive, is so absolutely essential to the schizoid compromise that for the therapist to interpret its function before the patient has developed an ability to create true relationships with real people is overwhelmingly threatening for the patient.

After obtaining consultation about the case, Mr. M.'s therapist began to interpret his massive fear of attack and his use of pornography and fantasy as his only semblance of a relationship with another person. Mr. M. resumed regular attendance in treatment, and over time gradually reduced his dependence on pornography as he was able to develop a stable and safe relationship with the therapist. He gradually began to take risks both within and outside of treatment, tentatively forming minimal relationships on the outside. After six years of treatment once a week, Mr. M. is still slowly emerging from his fantasy cocoon.

From *Split Self/Split Object: Understanding and Treating Borderline, Narcissistic, and Schizoid Disorders.* See page 196.

Philip Manfield, Ph.D., is a psychotherapist in the San Francisco East Bay area, where he has been in private practice and provided supervision and consultation for the past twenty-four years. His background and training are extremely eclectic and include gestalt, self psychology, and six years of training with the Masterson Institute.

28

Combining Psychotherapy with Pharmacotherapy

Gerald L. Klerman et al.

The major difficulties in combining drugs and psychotherapy do not lie in understanding the pharmacology of drugs or any of the specific problems in treatment. They have to do with patient and therapist attitudes.

American society is deeply divided about the efficacy, as well as the moral and social legitimacy, of drug treatment for emotional and psychiatric disorders. Nationwide surveys indicate that many patients who feel that they have been helped by tranquilizers and antidepressants, nevertheless report that they think drug therapy is less than the ideal way of coping with their emotional and psychological problems. There is a perva-

Gerald L.
Klerman

sive attitude that the use of medication is a crutch, that problems should be solved via self-reliance, personal initiative, and will power. It follows that efforts to get professional help for emotional and psychological problems are viewed as failure or weakness. Although this attitude has decreased dramatically in the past thirty years, it is still widespread.

Even patients who seek professional help for their emotional problems, including depression, tend to think that the most desirable way to deal with them is by psychological means, the gaining of insight and understanding. In this view, drug therapy is a second-class form of psychiatric treatment, reserved for individuals who are not capable of understanding and insight.

These views are mirrored within the mental health professions. Even among psychiatrists—the mental

health professionals who by training know most about medication and who are the only ones legally empowered to prescribe medications—there are deep splits over the value of drugs. Surveys indicate that the psychiatric profession is split in a number of different ways, and that one main factor dividing it is disagreement about whether drug therapy is effective and whether, even if it is effective, it is desirable. The psychiatrists who identify themselves as biological psychiatrists are a small but significant minority. Although they make up less than 20 percent of the members of the profession, they have gained considerable scientific and professional status because of advances in the development of new drugs and in the biological sciences in general. These advances have led to better

---

For a patient, a decision to take medication is often related to issues of dependence and independence, control of one's destiny, and sense of responsibility and power.

---

understanding of the pharmacology of drugs and the biochemical and physiological abnormalities that underlie some psychiatric disorders.

For therapists and patients alike, attitudes toward the use of medication not only involve larger social values but affect the meaning that the use of drugs has for the individual. For a patient, a decision to take medication is often related to issues of dependence and independence, control of one's destiny, and sense of responsibility and power.

These issues are illustrated in two contrasting case vignettes. Both involve adults who sought medication because of long-standing emotional problems after many years of psychotherapy of various sorts.

Arnold B., a forty-six-year-old male psychologist, had been very successful in his professional work but had a sense of frustration, low self-esteem, and personal inadequacy that had persisted since boyhood. Because of this he had never been successful in relationships with women and had remained unmarried. He had few friends except professional colleagues. Much of his satisfaction was tied up with his work as a member of a staff of a clinic associated with a university medical center. He and his father had spent many years in a chronic struggle: the son saw his father as intrusive and dominating of all the children but particularly himself. To separate himself from his father he went to graduate school and set up his practice two thousand miles from his family. Chronically frustrated and bitter, he had been in and out of various forms of psychotherapy since graduate school.

Soon after moving to Boston to join the faculty of a graduate school program, he sought psychiatric help because of the vegetative signs that had begun to accompany his chronic depression. He was also having early morning awakening and had developed a neck pain which was variously diagnosed as coming from cervical disc trouble or muscle tension. Although he himself raised the question as to whether or not med-

ication would be useful, he was extremely conflicted over the use of medicine, and only when
his neck problems became exacerbated and he
was having progressive early morning awakening did he request the use of a tricyclic. With 150
mg. of amitriptyline there was a rapid decrease
in the sleep difficulty and, more strikingly, in his
self-depreciation, bitterness, and frustration. His
attitude toward his parents, especially his father,
improved and he looked forward to visiting
them for the Christmas holidays in the hope of
working for a better relationship.

His attitude toward the success of the medication was one of a great deal of satisfaction
and a sense of having been relieved of a great

---

*He expressed a great deal of anger toward
previous therapists, raising the question as to whether
the use of medication earlier in his life might have
produced a happier and better adjustment.*

---

burden of guilt and self-depreciation that had
tormented him for many years. A month after
the symptoms had abated, he expressed a great
deal of anger toward previous therapists, raising
the question as to whether the use of medication earlier in his life might have produced a
happier and better adjustment.

With the subsidence of his symptoms he
began to work with his therapist on the question "What am I going to do for myself to make

myself happy, now that I'm grown-up and successful?"

Barbara W., a twenty-eight-year-old occupational therapist, had been working in the inpatient unit of a psychiatric hospital since her graduation from occupational therapy school and her internship. She had been in psychotherapy ever since her adolescence, when she began to have conflicts with her mother over such matters as choice of dress and selection of boyfriends. As long as she could remember she and her mother had been locked in a struggle for control, the patient resisting the mother's attempts to influence her life. The patient saw these efforts as domineering, representing the mother's attempt to live vicariously through her daughter's social, sexual, and occupational achievements.

Mrs. W. had been married for a number of years and had one small child. Although the child was developing well, she was tormented by the feeling that she was not giving enough to the child and that the amount of time she spent in her professional work made her less attentive toward her family. Although the marriage had been turbulent ever since their courtship, her husband, an engineer, had at first refused to consider marital treatment, feeling that if they worked hard enough on their problems they could find some solution themselves. While Barbara was in individual therapy, their sexual adjustment had improved considerably and her husband agreed to couple therapy. She described her husband as very satisfied sexually, although she herself was not always capable of reaching orgasm.

The patient came for possible medication on the suggestion of her psychotherapist, who had been seeing her and her husband in couple therapy for a number of years. Although the quality of the relationship between the patient and her husband had improved considerably, the therapist noted that she still had a low-grade depression, a sense of low self-esteem and self-depreciation out of proportion to her actual life circumstance and to her genuine accomplishments as a professional and as a mother and wife.

The patient was started on imipramine, 125 mg. a day, and within a week reported a decrease in her low self-esteem and a particular sense of increased vitality and activity level. This increased zest for life and activity made her question whether she was having a hypomanic episode and whether she was basically bipolar.

On the one hand, she was extremely pleased with the relief of her distress and the sense of energy, competence, and accomplishment that developed during the weeks after she began medication. On the other, she felt she had lost control over her emotions. She had always prided herself on the hope that if she gained sufficient understanding and insight she could master her emotional state and control her feelings as well as her life circumstances. To her the use of medication represented a challenge to her aspiration for self-mastery. It suggested that some parts of her destiny might be controlled not by her wishes and understanding but by some biochemical imbalance in her central nervous system.

These two cases illustrate the conflict and ambivalence in our society in general and in the mental health professions in particular about the use of medication in psychotherapy. For the first patient, the medication brought relief; his feeling was, "Now I don't have to feel responsible for what happened to me." In contrast, the second patient felt the medication took away from her the possibility of determining her own destiny.

From *Interpersonal Psychotherapy of Depression: A Brief, Focused, Specific Strategy.* See page 196.

The late Gerald L. Klerman, M.D., was Professor of Psychiatry at Cornell Medical Center in New York City.

Myrna M. Weissman, Ph.D., is Professor of Epidemiology in Psychiatry, College of Physicians and Surgeons of Columbia University.

Bruce J. Rounsaville, M.D., is Associate Professor of Psychiatry at the Yale University School of Medicine.

Eve S. Chevron, M.S., was the Project Coordinator at the Depression Research Unit at the Yale University School of Medicine.

*Information about suicide
emerges readily if asked for.*

29

Evaluation of Suicidal Potentiality

Robert E. Litman

Persons who are considering suicide as a potential solution to life crises seek out physicians, hoping for answers less extreme than suicide. Although 75 percent of suicides had seen a physician within 6 months of the death, unfortunately, patients do not ordinarily reveal spontaneously that they are in suicidal crises. This information emerges readily, however, if the physician asks for it, especially if there is a preexisting patient–physician relationship of confidence and trust. When he notes prodromal clues to suicide, the physician must decide how to proceed.

Usually, the most tactful and informative technique is to approach the suicidal motivation gradually through a series of questions, working from the more general to the most specific. Such a series of questions might proceed in this manner: "How is your life going?

How are you feeling in general? How are your spirits—your mental outlook—your hopes?" If the answers indicate low spirits or pessimistic attitudes or much tension or confusion, another series of questions might follow: "Do you wish you could be out of it? Would you like sometimes to give up? Ever wish you were dead?"

If the answers to the above are suggestively affirmative, then the physician might pose a third series of questions: "Have you thought of ending your life? How close are you now to suicide? How would you do it? What is your plan?"

Suicide Plan

The most important single element in evaluating the immediate suicide emergency is the patient's suicide plan, including the proposed method, place, and

time. If the patient has decided upon a specific, highly lethal method of suicide with an instrument that is readily available to him, there is a serious emergency. Usually, patients will talk to an interested physician about the details of their suicide plans, although sometimes this information is obtained from friends or relatives. We take it seriously when a patient sets a deadline for his action; for instance, his fiftieth birthday, retirement day, or an anniversary. Vague suicide plans are somewhat reassuring, as are plans to use methods of relatively low lethality, such as aspirin ingestion.

Direct denials are usually truthful and can be relied on, at least temporarily. "Yes, I thought of suicide, but I would never do it because of my children." "For me, suicide is impossible because of my religion." "I would leave town first." The exceptions to this rule—that is,

Suicidal crises vary in emergency force, according to the patient's character.

patients who dissemble to friendly physicians—are nearly always obvious psychiatric cases, usually with a history of psychiatric hospitalization.

Physicians who hesitate to ask such direct questions about suicide because of possible harmful effects on patients should be reassured by the experience of the staff of the Suicide Prevention Center in Los Angeles. In interviews with ten thousand suicidal patients and reviews of three thousand suicide deaths, we found no evidence that such questions had ever harmed patients.

Severity of Symptoms

Danger signals include: severe agitation with depression; helplessness, combined with a frantic need to do something; hopelessness that gets worse in response to helping efforts from others; confusion; paranoid trends with persecution delusions or homicidal threats. Five percent of suicidal patients are also potentially homicidal.

Basic Personality

Suicidal crises vary in emergency force, according to the patient's character. Persons who have led stable, responsible lives generally respond well to treatment and return to their previous levels. Because of the favorable prognosis, such persons should be the objects of extremely zealous suicide prevention

efforts. At present about half of the persons who kill themselves are of that order. Sometimes high social position, public prominence, or professional success is a barrier between patients and the help they need. Examples are physicians, military leaders, and political figures. (Many lives would be saved if persons in crises could accept help without stigma.)

By contrast, many unstable, immature, addictive, alcoholic, and deviant persons are chronically on the edge of self-destruction. These patients benefit less from emergency first aid. They need consistent firm direction and long-range rehabilitation.

Precipitating Stress

If the suicidal crisis is a reaction to an overwhelming, sudden stress, the patient needs emergency protection and support but may recover rapidly and spontaneously. This is analogous to heat stroke collapse. If the suicidal crisis represents an internal decompensation with no special external stress, the patient may need special study and special treatment, presumably by a psychiatrist. This is analogous to a physiological crisis due to adrenal cortical insufficiency.

Resources

These include physical, financial, and interpersonal assets. The willingness and ability of other persons to aid the patient often makes the difference between life and death. Some patients are emotionally bankrupt, and this must be taken into account. For example, many alcoholics, after years of self-destructive behavior that has alienated family and friends, hit bottom and are highly suicidal.

Special Indicators

These include such factors as family history of suicide, recent suicide of a close friend or relative, anniversary of a divorce or of a death in the family, complete social isolation, history of psychiatric treatment, especially recent discharge from a mental hospital, and recent suicide attempt, unrecognized or untreated.

From *The Psychology of Suicide: A Clinician's Guide to Evaluation and Treatment.* See page 197.

Robert E. Litman, M.S., M.D., Ph.D., is Clinical Professor of Psychiatry at the UCLA School of Medicine. Dr. Litman helphed found the Los Angeles Suicide Prevention Center and was Chief Psychiatrist of the Center for more than thirty years.

30

Use of the Telephone as a Transitional Space

Joyce K. Aronson

A dangerously ill anorexic began therapy and became so afraid of her needs—of what might be aroused in the contact between us, the possible threat to her schizoid withdrawal into anorexic preoccupation, and her unconscious fear of the inevitable disappointments in our potential intima-cy—that she refused to come in to see me. However, she discovered the use of telephone sessions and the answering machine as a transitional space.

Joyce K. Aronson

Interpretations were meaningless to this patient. For example, I could tell her that she wanted to have me endlessly, but it had no effect. She needed to enact it for a mutual engagement to evolve. Since she found a face-to-face encounter

153

overwhelming, the following parameters were used: permitting telephone sessions, allowing the therapist's telephone answering machine to be used as a transitional space, letting her limit the time of sessions and set limits on the therapist's affect, being available to help the patient deal with the immediate and overwhelming anxiety aroused as she tried new experiences, avoiding hospitalization insofar as there was no threat to life, and having telephone contact during vacations for the first four years of treatment. Each parameter became unnecessary as the patient grew emotionally.

Initially she came to some sessions, although very late. She had a difficult time just organizing her daily life, shopping, eating, and getting to my office. Terrified of the unexpected, she was totally preoccupied with others' perceptions of her, and often heard accusing voices saying, "She's an anorexic." Because

of her father's treatment of her, she expected rageful responses if she asked for anything.

In this beginning phase, she talked about her love of skating, and gradually, with enormous anxiety and fear of criticism for being too thin and not being perfect, she started taking skating lessons again. Terrified of any new experiences, she would come home flooded with feelings and leave lengthy messages on my answering machine. She was obsessed with being criticized, felt people could read her mind, were calling her sick and anorexic, and were silently denigrating her skating.

As a therapist, what I said did not matter as much as what I did. I had to be available as much as possible to maintain the illusion of constant availability. I did not charge for phone time since I was being paid my full fee for three sessions a week. She needed to feel that I wanted to talk to her for nothing in order to maintain the sense that I cared for her—a prerequisite for the relationship. She later spoke of her skating instructors, who stayed with her a few minutes more at the end of her lesson, as possibly caring. Eventually I addressed this in the transference. Initially, and for several years, it was essential to the treatment that this illusion of caring availability, which she had never experienced with her mother, be enacted over a long period of time.

I had to be able to live through her pain, despair, depression, self-destructiveness, and demandingness. It became apparent that the major affective response from her parents was related to her illness. They came running when she was hospitalized, although expressing rage that she was ill. After years of illness, when she gave a public performance, preparing months in advance and telling them about it, the parents not only didn't come, but didn't even ask her about it.

When she started to come to full sessions about three years after treatment began, I found myself dreading our meetings. In anticipation of seeing her, I wanted to eat something to store up energy so I wouldn't feel depleted. I had the fear that I wouldn't be able to get rid of her. I felt burdened, tired, as if I'd be drained. This countertransference feeling put me in touch with her voracious neediness for human contact, which she had been keeping at bay.

In this situation we can see the way in which a carefully planned parameter can be usefully employed to advance the treatment of certain patients. This patient's use of the telephone answering machine allowed her to speak to me as if I were present and as

---

In this transitional space she could accept therapy while rejecting it, accept the therapeutic relationship while at the same time rejecting the terrifying closeness to another person.

---

if I were her omnipotent creation. It served as a transitional object that was not suggested by me. It was found by the patient, arising out of her deep, unmet needs and enabled her to build up an internal object. As she became able to talk to me in her mind, her voices disappeared.

Transitional objects are used, as the telephone was

in this case, in the development of reality acceptance. In this transitional space she could accept therapy while rejecting it, accept the therapeutic relationship while at the same time rejecting the terrifying closeness to another person. Just as a transitional object becomes unnecessary and is relinquished in the course of development, in time this patient no longer needed to use the telephone as a transitional space.

From *Use of the Telephone in Psychotherapy*. See page 197.

Joyce K. Aronson, Ph.D., is on the faculty of the Center for the Study of Anorexia and Bulimia and is in private practice in New York City.

31

Treatment of Patients with Agoraphobia

Pat Sable

Agoraphobia is defined as fear of leaving familiar surroundings, especially when alone. Symptoms vary from person to person, with the fears of venturing out alone and into strange and distant areas the two most dreaded situations. These symptoms are frequently part of a cluster of fears that may include going into public places such as crowded theaters or shopping centers; traveling in a train, bus, or car; and being in open or closed spaces or in high places. Fear tends to be associated with specific situations such as standing in line, being on a bridge, or driving on the freeway, where a quick escape to a familiar location is difficult or impossible. The person may fear that something dreadful will happen while

Pat
Sable

158

he or she is away from home, something such as dying or becoming helpless. Moreover, the more anxious a person becomes, the more fears of leaving home are magnified. Sometimes the feared situations are social, such as fear of visibly trembling or being stared at.

When children are prohibited from expressing anxiety, anger, or sadness, they may selectively exclude experiences or feelings that would elicit attachment behavior. As a consequence, an adult client may not only have difficulty identifying and expressing emotions, but also identifying the family situations that may have produced them. This defensive exclusion manifests in treatment when clients are reluctant to rely on their therapists or have difficulty communicating their feelings. A crucial part of therapy, then, is for the therapist to become a trusted companion whose skills help the client feel really heard and adequately understood.

Fear of separation and anxiety about the reliability of others were central issues in my work with Megan and in my attempt to help her discover the nature of her family experiences. Her feelings of anxious attachment in relationships led her to impose certain expectations on her therapist that were clarified as they were elicited in the transference relationship. For example, Megan worried about displeasing her therapist, and tried to accommodate to what she thought might be demanded of her. She also tried to be the strong one by excluding her own feelings. It was suggested that she might be afraid she would lose the support of her therapist if she let her know she was sometimes angry with her.

Her feelings of anxious attachment in relationships led her to impose certain expectations on her therapist.

As therapy progressed and Megan began to feel secure with her therapist, she could look at her responses, such as the fear and anger that were evoked upon threat of separation or disappointment in relationships. She brought her mother, sister, and two different male friends with her to sessions, which made it possible to directly observe their behavior and their interactions with Megan. Her therapist proposed that this might also be a way for Megan to expose the way she was treated by others so that her therapist would then validate her impressions. This also helped show Megan how difficult it was to simply express herself to her family. When her mother attended a session, she proclaimed her affection for Megan amid a mixture of complaints, for instance, that Megan needed to be "less childish" and "more independent."

Subsequent to this hour, Megan had begun to see that in spite of what her mother said, she had held her daughter in the position of caregiver for herself. Her mother's confusing messages, which conveyed that Megan was strong but also dependent, became apparent. Megan began to understand how she had misconstrued her mother's caregiving behavior and to comprehend the origin of her anxious attachment to her mother and to others. She was more able to retrieve and review experiences and feelings that she had excluded for a long time. For example, she thought she

---

Megan had begun to see that in spite of what her mother said, she had held her daughter in the position of caregiver for herself.

---

provoked conflict in relationships because she feared the other person would stop seeing her and because she wanted reassurance. About this time, Megan moved into her own apartment. She also began to have steadier attachments with men, though at first with men who did not treat her well. One of them, Steven, attended several sessions with Megan. She had decided he was not the kind of man with whom she wanted a committed relationship and wanted to leave him, but found she had become afraid to be away from him, afraid to be alone, and that her driving problems had returned. These were all indications of her anxious attachment.

Gradually, Megan's real attachment experiences became clearer to her and she came to understand how her family had affected her confidence in forming satisfactory relationships. She ended the relationship with Steven and changed some of her behavior with her mother.

The therapeutic relationship of attachment provided Megan with a safe base from which she began to examine and sort out a lifetime of experiences. It was significant for her that she was not made to feel overdependent, but that her behavior was seen as a reasonable response to the way she had been treated in her family, not only in the past but also in the present.

From *Attachment and Adult Psychotherapy*. See page 197.

Pat Sable, Ph.D., is Adjunct Associate Professor at the University of Southern California School of Social Work. She also maintains a private psychotherapy practice and has lectured and written extensively on the application of attachment theory to clinical practice with adults.

> *We must face and own*
> *the deepest versions of our reality.*

32

Sexual Complaints Mask Our Deepest Wishes

Alan Bell

Sexual counseling, if it is ever to be successful, requires more than anything else an uncommon honesty on the part of the individuals involved, the therapist as well as the client. Those who are party to this enterprise must get to the point where they can speak their minds and own their most secret agendas, risk shame and embarrassment in a monumental effort to make themselves known to themselves and to the others, and declare their bottom lines.

For the therapist, this might involve insisting that the couple carry out the tasks agreed upon and refusing to meet again until the couple has made good on their promise. At times he may have to call a spade a spade no matter how

Alan Bell

much this may generate discomfort in the couple: the therapist who is unwilling to risk animus from one or both partners in the effort to redefine the problem or to change the old rules of the partnership will never get the job done. As much as anything else the therapist must model "real talk," be appropriately assertive, and remain confident that no matter what occurs during a clinical exchange, no matter what "mistakes" are made, they can always be rectified if they are ultimately processed and shared.

For the clients, bottom lines will involve taking clear stands with their partners and sometimes with the therapist, declaring what they are willing and not willing to do in behalf of the relationship. Most of all, they must come to see that personal integrity is far more important than interpersonal harmony, that self-respect counts for more than smiles on another's face.

Transparency will probably remain the chief challenge of our lives, never entirely accomplished, given our histories of learned evasiveness. We should rejoice in those moments when we struggle to allow ourselves to be known without apology.

It would appear that all too often behavioral prescriptions are simply not enough to get couples off dead center. Far more important are efforts that must be made to uncover each individual partner's personal truths. These form the bedrock of all that occurs in the sexual domain. It is here, in the mind and heart, that sexual needs and interests and torments can be more clearly understood, and only then, sometimes, changed.

- What does your sexuality mean to you, what is its purpose, how does it fit into your life, what part would you have it play in your partnership?
- How do you understand the importance or lack of importance you assign to sexual intimacy?
- What goes on in you at various junctures of your sexual exchanges: What are you feeling, what are you thinking, what do you wish?

According to psychodynamic formulations, oftentimes our chief complaint masks our deepest wish, and it is the latter that must be owned and understood before any progress can be made. Sometimes, with or without the help of a therapist, such radical inquiry into the heart and mind can be conducted by completing a full sentence such as, "If, all of a sudden, I found myself full of sexual interest and eager for my mate, it is possible that. . . ." The woman with a lack of sexual interest must do far more than wring her hands; she must pursue her various ideational trails to uncover the array of consequences more dreadful than those she now struggles with. Suppose one is the fear that if she were to awaken her sexual interest she might become sexually promiscuous: One strategy would be for her to write down on a 3 x 5 card, "As much as I suffer from my lack of sexual interest, I'd rather live with it than run the risk of becoming a whore, and I shall make sure to avoid

---

If and when we can daily face and own the deepest versions of our reality, we can make a conscious choice to change or to stay the same.

---

this risk by doing all I can to control myself sexually." This woman has followed her ideational trail to identify a focal construct—an important concept that is part of her emotional reality. By writing it on a card, along with other constructs on other cards, she acknowledges that it exists for her: "This is me. This is part of who I am."

If and when we can daily face and own the deepest versions of our reality, we can make a conscious choice to change or to stay the same. It is up to us, we are ready, and at least we know where we are. We are no longer trying to get someplace with no good idea of where on the map we are starting from. We confront our profound ambivalence and recognize parts of ourselves at odds with each other, each fostering its own version of reality. ("I know this in my head, but not in my gut.") Intellectual truths and emotional truths are often not the same, but until the differences become clearer to us, until both are embraced equally, we "can't get there from here." This may be especially so in the sexual domain, where the stakes feel so high, where there are major consequences for how we conduct ourselves, and where we keep our deepest convictions about what is possible or necessary.

From *The Mind and Heart in Human Sexual Behavior: Owning and Sharing Our Personal Truths.* See page 198.

Alan Bell, Ph.D., is Professor Emeritus in the Department of Counseling Psychology at Indiana University and practices psychotherapy in Bloomington, Indiana.

> *Men with sexual problems and*
> *what women can do to help them.*

33

Resolving Trouble in the Bedroom

Eva Margolies

What are the chances that you or a woman you know will encounter a man with a sexual problem? Although there are no definitive statistics, there is every reason to believe that the woman who has not encountered such a man is the exception. Recent studies estimate that about 30 percent of all men suffer from premature ejaculation and another 10 percent suffer from erectile dysfunctions, the new euphemism for impotence.

Most women do not know that men with premature ejaculation are not sexually selfish but are completely unable to control their orgasms. Nor are most women aware that erection problems, particularly at the beginning

Eva
Margolies

168

of a new relationship, are almost never a sign of a man's lack of attraction for his partner. And the majority of women are completely oblivious of the thousands of thirty-, forty-, and even fifty-year-old men who suffer from sexual shyness and inexperience. Indeed, the high-powered, single CEO who constantly rejects the advances of women is possibly suffering from some sort of sexual problem or feelings of inadequacy.

The most difficult thing of all for a man with sexual problems to believe, however, is that any woman, even one he has been in a long-term relationship with, can respect a man with any sort of sexual problem. It does not matter how good-looking he is or how much money he makes. A man with a sexual problem believes that he is seriously defective as a male, and he projects those feelings onto everyone around him.

By far the primary cause of impotence in men is worry about having an erection. A man can lose his erection for all sorts of reasons. Whatever actually triggers the problem, however, the anxiety that a man develops around the issue is what keeps it going and over time can actually become its number one cause.

While some men develop erection problems because they are out of touch with their bodies, there is a whole slew of men whose penises stop

---

*These men have bought society's view that a man
is supposed to function with any woman
regardless of his feelings about her.*

---

working because they are out of touch with what is going on in their heads. These men have bought society's view that a man is supposed to function with any woman regardless of his feelings about her or his relationship with her. Believing that men are sex machines, such a man assumes that his penis should be ready, willing, and able whenever there is an available female in the vicinity and that he should perform sexually regardless of circumstances.

Considering how devastated a man feels when he suffers from impotence, it is amazing how easily the overwhelming majority of cases can be solved under the right circumstances. Like the man with premature ejaculation, a man with nonorganic impotence needs to learn how to relax and focus on the physical sensations he is feeling in his body. This helps reduce the performance anxiety that is a staple among all men with impotence, as well as gives a man a consistent, physical basis for arousal that he can count on. The feeling of mental turn-on that can produce a firm sustainable erection in a man of twenty-five is no longer sufficient to the job as he gets older. But if he can focus on good feelings in his body and receives adequate stimulation, he will learn to trust his body once again to respond adequately.

If there is any one motto that summarizes the strategy for resolving most sexual problems, it is this: Think less and feel more. Whether a man has premature ejaculation, impotence, desire, or orgasm problems, there is so much noise in his head that he can't focus on what he is feeling in his body. This inability to concentrate on the present is a cornerstone of almost all sexual dysfunctions. Learning to get out of his head by tuning in to his body is the first step in successfully overcoming them.

This approach is called sensate focus. It is a very powerful tool. Staying in touch with the pleasurable physical sensations of the moment curbs the tendency of the mind to run ahead of the body, a problem found frequently among men with PE and erection problems. Being able to respond to good feelings in his body also gives a man who doesn't feel strong desire or sexual passion a way of functioning sexually. Finally, focusing on the present helps alleviate performance anxiety. If a man's attention is focused on *what* he is doing, he will worry less about *how* he is doing.

How can you help your partner to recover? His chances are excellent if:

1. *You are willing to reconcile your ignorance with*

the facts. Since a great many problems are created by overreacting to or simply not knowing about the predictable, normal changes that occur in a man's penis as he ages, accepting the reality of sexual development can make all the difference in the world.

2. *You are willing to be sexually giving and provide adequate stimulation.* If the problem is a need for more physical contact, the cure is simple enough. If you are too inhibited or selfish to give your partner sufficient genital stimulation, the problem is yours, not his.

3. *You are able to have orgasms in other ways besides intercourse and do not feel that coitus is the be-all and end-all of lovemaking.* If a man can feel reassured that he doesn't need a hard penis to keep you sexually content, a lot of his performance pressure will be reduced. This naturally makes the chances for successful intercourse much greater.

Erections are, for a man, as much a matter of the mind as of the body. A caring, educated partner is the best medicine.

From *Men with Sexual Problems and What Women Can Do to Help Them.* See page 198.

Eva Margolies, M.A., C.S.T., is certified by the American Association of Sex Educators, Counselors, and Therapists. She is Director of the Center for Sexual Recovery in New York City and the author of four books on women, men, and sexuality.

> *The more severe the psychopathic disturbance,*
> *the more likely psychotherapy will fail.*

34
Psychotherapy of the Psychopath

J. Reid Meloy

The premise of treatment is to heal. It incorporates an attitude of caring, empathy, and optimism for the eventual well-being of the patient. This is fundamentally different from the premise of evaluation, particularly forensic evaluation, wherein the purpose is to gather valid and reliable information to address certain psycholegal questions. I have found this to be an area of confusion, especially for beginning professionals who are defining their roles as clinicians and do not, as yet, have the experience to shift smoothly from one attitude to another. Clarifying roles is necessary, if not crucial, to the treatment of psychopathically disturbed individuals because of the inclination of these patients to deceive others.

J. Reid Meloy

173

Mental health professionals, whether they be psychologists, psychiatrists, or social workers, are implicitly taught throughout their training to believe what patients tell them. This is supportive of the role of healing, but it is very unrealistic in a forensic context where deception may be characterologically expectable or institutionally reinforced. Psychologists or psychiatrists functioning as forensic investigators know this and will make allowances for deception through careful corroboration of their data. In fact, my assumption in doing forensic work is that the individual being evaluated will deceive me and therefore I must disprove my hypothesis to arrive at the truth. This is a safe and reasonable way to approach forensic psychological investigations, but it is sometimes antithetical to psychotherapy.

Psychopathically disturbed individuals being con-

sidered for psychotherapy consequently present a dilemma: they should be believed, yet the prediction is that they will deceive. There is no simple answer to this conundrum, and the psychotherapist who has made the conscious decision to treat, rather than evaluate, the psychopathically disturbed patient must recognize both his or her commitment to healing and honesty and the nature of the character disturbance to be treated. The conscious tolerance of these ambiguities will inoculate the clinician against the countertransference impulse to polarize, split off, and devalue the psychopathically disturbed patient as untreatable.

The therapist who decides to treat the psychopath must recognize both the commitment to healing and honesty, and the nature of the character disturbance.

I have emphasized that psychopathy is a deviant developmental process that is manifest as a disturbance of personality function. From a treatment perspective it is most usefully conceptualized on a hypothetical continuum, ranging from mild to severe. This premise is particularly important for avoiding the already-noted countertransference reaction to psychopathy: the patient is a psychopath, therefore he is untreatable. Here the clinician has fallen prey to his own disidentifying and dehumanizing impulse, a predictable, and common, reaction to psychopathy.

The clinical perspective of human behavior as continuous, rather than dichotomous, is more amenable to psychotherapeutic formulations. I think it is also more representative of actual reality, and it is important in refining our understanding of psychopathic disturbance.

The more severe the psychopathic disturbance, the more likely psychotherapy will fail. The severity of psychopathic disturbance also dictates the necessary restrictiveness of the treatment approach; for example, mild psychopathically disturbed patients may benefit from weekly individual psychotherapy, in contrast to severe psychopathically disturbed patients who will need a highly structured inpatient milieu to derive any treatment benefits.

Treatability of psychopathically disturbed individuals correlates with their capacity to form attachments and their degree of superego pathology. Both characteristics should be assessed to determine the least restrictive environment within which treatment will be attempted.

The capacity to form attachments is related to the degree to which the patient can form a genuine emotional relationship to the psychotherapist regardless of the transference distortion within that relationship. Such an internal representational world would predict a capacity to attach, albeit in a self-effacing and masochistic manner, and would suggest a more ambivalent relationship to the internal stranger selfobject. These patients would be better candidates for psychotherapy.

From *The Psychopathic Mind: Origins, Dynamics, and Treatment.* See page 198.

J. Reid Meloy, Ph.D., is a diplomate in forensic psychology of the American Board of Professional Psychology and now devotes his time to a private civil and criminal forensic practice, research, writing, and teaching.

35

Assessing and Treating Criminals

Stanton E. Samenow

Among mental health professionals, good intentions abound, but many are ill-equipped to assess and treat antisocial individuals. There are several reasons for this.

One reason is the tendency among mental health professionals to focus on causes. Mistakenly, they believe that if they understand the origin of the behavior, they can better treat it. In the effort to understand, they seek to unearth causative factors by exploring childhood experiences. The criminal is all too ready to assist us in that endeavor. The search for reasons why and the treatment based on those alleged causes invariably result in criminals developing psychological "insight," but

Stanton E. Samenow

remaining criminals. The type of insight developed by criminals when treated by well-meaning, but uninformed, counselors and therapists should be spelled "incite." The offender is incited to blame people and forces outside himself, most of which he never would have thought of on his own.

Mental health professionals who help patients suffering from depression and low self-esteem mistakenly believe that these are the key problems that plague offenders. Certain obvious facts attest to the antisocial person's failures throughout his life. He may be an outcast from his family, uneducated, a dropout from the workforce, and an individual who never has supported himself. Unless the antisocial person has a long record that is known to the mental health worker, he does not wear a badge proclaiming his criminality.

Meeting his new patient or client in a detention center, hospital, or clinic, the therapist is likely to encounter a deeply distressed human being. He is likely to see his mission as helping his patient develop insight, feel better, and regard himself positively. The therapist approaches this task with empathy and understanding. In working with a criminal, these objectives all are counterproductive because they are based on erroneous premises. The criminal is depressed about his circumstances, not about himself. No matter how he seems to others, he does not regard himself as a failure. Rather than being rejected, the offender is the one who has done the rejecting, by turning his back on family, school, work, and others who tried to exert a positive influence. He will regard

---

The criminal is depressed about his circumstances, not about himself.

---

the compassionate therapist as a sucker and take advantage of him. His overriding aim is to escape from his disagreeable situation of the moment, not to improve himself.

Applying psychological approaches that work with most patient populations results in criminals sophisticated in psychology rather than criminals without psychology. They remain criminals. So long as the change agent fails to recognize that, in the criminal, he is dealing with virtually a different breed of human being, he cannot be effective. He may inadvertently "enable" the behavior to persist.

Gullibility and cynicism both are counselor errors. The person new to working with criminals wants to believe what his client or patient is telling him. The criminal adroitly feeds a gullible therapist what he thinks the therapist wants to hear. Speaking of his former therapist, one offender recalled, "When I satisfied her theory, I was cured." The therapist had concluded that the offender's cruel treatment of females stemmed from long festering anger toward his mother who, he claimed, had treated him abusively. However, the offender failed to disclose that his mother was harsh only with him; she was very lenient with his brother and sister because they were easy to raise. They had excelled academically, worked during summers and diligently saved money, then attended college and prepared for careers. In stark contrast, the criminal headed down a different path. His mother wanted to trust him, just as she had trusted her other children, but he betrayed her trust. She found clothes and cassette tapes in his room that she knew she had not purchased and that he could not have paid for by himself. She received calls from neighborhood parents and school teachers about his picking fights with other children. He told her he had no homework when some had been assigned, and he feigned illness so he could stay home from school. When things did not go his way at home, he became extremely belligerent, sometimes destroying property. His mother responded by imposing restrictions, taking away privileges, refusing to sign for him to get a driver's license, grounding him, and doing just about anything else she could think of to try to teach him to be more responsible, to keep him safe, and to prevent him from throwing opportunities away.

The story the therapist received was of a child who got a raw deal from a mother who was mean, arbitrary, and played favorites with his two siblings. In session after session, the offender emphasized what his mother "did" to him, but he revealed very little of his own misconduct. The therapist believed that his physical and emotional mistreatment of girlfriends and, later, his wife, stemmed from his long suppressed rage toward an authoritarian, unsympathetic mother, which was being displaced onto all women in his adult life. The offender convinced the therapist that he had improved because he had gained this insight and therefore no longer harbored this buried anger. She was preparing to discharge him from treatment when, much to her shock and dismay, he again beat up his wife.

The criminal quickly marks the gullible agent of change as an easy target to manipulate. The therapist believes his patient is being truthful and progressing. When the offender reverts to old patterns, the therapist grows disillusioned and, if this happens frequently enough with clients, quite cynical.

Although the opposite of gullibility, unbridled cynicism also imposes a formidable obstacle to effective work with this population. One must think of it from the offender's point of view. Who would like to confide deeply personal matters in a counselor who never seems to believe one word? Such a relationship would deteriorate quickly.

For agents of change working with criminals, it is

necessary to avoid both gullibility and cynicism. By adopting a "time will tell" attitude, the change agent does not feel impelled to make an on-the-spot judgment as to the offender's credibility when he has no way of knowing at the time what the truth actually is. Eventually, the facts will emerge.

From *Straight Talk About Criminals: Understanding and Treating Antisocial Individuals.* See page 199.

Stanton E. Samenow, Ph.D., specializes in the evaluation and treatment of juvenile and adult offenders.

Appendix

**THE PRIMITIVE EDGE
OF EXPERIENCE** (sc)
Thomas H. Ogden
0-87668-290-5, $40.00

"In this magnificent book, Ogden illuminates the darkest recesses of the human psyche with his brilliant formulation of the autistic-contiguous position. He also provides refreshing new perspectives on the Oedipus complex and female psychology. With this impressive contribution, Thomas Ogden has come into his own as one of the most creative and original psychoanalytic thinkers of our time." —Glen O. Gabbard

**OPENING GAMBITS: The First
Session of Psychotherapy**
Peter S. Armstrong
0-7657-0241-X, $40.00

"The first session of psycho-therapy is crucial. It sets up expectations for the kind of treatment that is to follow, and if not well conducted, it may be the last session. Challenging experienced therapists to examine their own habits, Peter Armstrong also guides beginners through the opportunities and pitfalls of this surprisingly neglected subject."
—George Pigman

**EVOCATIVENESS:
Moving and Persuasive
Interventions in Psychotherapy**
Stephen A. Appelbaum
0-7657-0246-0, $45.00

"In a step-by-step fashion, Appelbaum elucidates the 'art' of psychotherapy. He delineates what is fresh, deeply felt, authentic, and poignant in the therapist's communications and the ways in which such evocativeness impacts the patient. Appelbaum's work is a most unusual confluence of Freud, ego psychology, Winnicott, Bion, acting, poetry, linguistics, fiction, and so many other unexpected ingredients. A deeply moving and clinically indispensable contribution indeed!" —Salman Akhtar

DEEPENING THE TREATMENT
Jane S. Hall
0-7657-0176-6, $40.00
"Jane Hall describes a special kind of respect for the patient and the latent meanings of the patient's manifest utterances, and stresses the use of the transference as a prime tool in deepening the treatment. The book is especially welcome as a balance to the proliferation of therapies that overlook the unconscious." —Gertrude Blanck

pist in the therapeutic encounter as on the dynamic changes that occur in the patient. The author's uncanny knack for conveying the sense of the larger unity of a dyadic relationship that arises from the interchange between the treater and the treated gives the reader a profound insight into the processes taking place on both sides of the equation. Dr. Roth goes far beyond simply describing the techniques of psychotherapy: he teaches not merely how to do therapy, but how to be a therapist."
—John C. Nemiah

OBJECT RELATIONS INDIVIDUAL THERAPY (sc)
Jill Scharff & David E. Scharff
0-7657-0251-7, $50.00
"Arguably the finest contemporary teachers of object relations theory, Drs. Jill and David Scharff have put their teaching in writing in what must certainly be the most comprehensive text to date. It is thoughtfully organized and strikes a fine balance between theory and practice; readers can trust the Scharffs' accounts of others' work.

PSYCHOTHERAPY:
The Art of Wooing Nature (sc)
Sheldon Roth
0-7657-0252-5, $35.00
"Reading Dr. Roth's book is like being in therapy with a highly skilled, empathic, and creative analyst. The focus is as much on the experience of the thera-

The book's unparalleled accomplishment lies in the quality of the clinical writing, especially in their authors' accounts of their own passing states of mind—or countertransferences—in work with their patients. A truly fine book."

—Christopher Bollas

EMPATHIC ATTUNEMENT:
The "Technique" of Psychoanalytic
Self Psychology (sc)
Crayton E. Rowe Jr. &
David S. Mac Isaac
0-87668-551-3, $40.00

"The authors take beginners by the hand and walk them through the details of the contributions of Heinz Kohut in a simple, direct, masterly, and easy-to-follow fashion. They have digested Kohut's work, made it their own, and, through their clinical examples, sensitively bring their readers step-by-step inside their clinical experiences. They share this in an open, sound, and pedagogically appealing fashion. They are as empathic with their readers as they are with their patients—a most felicitous combination."

—Paul Ornstein

THERAPEUTIC ACTION:
A Guide to
Psychoanalytic Therapy
Enrico E. Jones
0-7657-0243-6, $60.00

"A masterful achievement! A genuine integration of systematic observation with the art of clinical practice, this is an invaluable book to guide all therapists, the experienced and the novice, through the troubled waters of psychodynamic treatment. I cannot imagine anyone who reads this book not becoming a more effective therapist as a consequence."

—Peter Fonagy

**CONVERSATIONS AT THE
FRONTIER OF DREAMING**
Thomas H. Ogden
0-7657-0312-2, $40.00

Dr. Thomas Ogden is the most widely read and creative psycho-analyst writing today. This, his most important book, is on how one thinks and works as an analyst; how to increase the capacity to feel in a visceral way the alive moments of a session; and how, through close attention to the nuances of language, gestures, and actions, to grasp the intersubjective construction the patient and the therapist are creating. Ogden uses reverie—waking dreams—a process in which metaphors are created, to achieve a sense of unconscious experience.

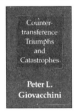

**COUNTERTRANSFERENCE TRIUMPHS
AND CATASTROPHES** (sc)
Peter L. Giovacchini
0-87668-284-0, $60.00

"This is a splendid teaching tool, combining scholarship with clinical gems that demonstrate Dr. Giovacchini's concept of counter-transference and the part it plays in treatment. Although he discusses the disturbances countertransference can cause, he shows how the proper handling of this phenomenon enhances the good outcomes.

"Analysts and psychotherapists will return to this book again and again over the years to seek inner guidance in their clinical work. I, for one, would like it to be at hand at all times."
—Vamık D. Volkan

**BRIEF THERAPY: Short-Term
Psychodynamic Intervention** (sc)
Gregory P. Bauer & Joseph C. Kobos
1-56821-102-3, $50.00

"*Brief Therapy* is a valuable addition to the burgeoning literature on time-limited psychotherapy. The authors competently summarize and integrate the major writings in this field. The book is a model of clarity and the clinical vignettes are well-chosen. The volume is highly recommended to practicing therapists who wish to augment their expertise in short-term therapy as well as to students who are interested in a balanced overview. The briefer forms of dynamic psychotherapy have achieved new respectability and they are bound to have a bright future."

—Hans H. Strupp

DYNAMIC PSYCHOTHERAPY:
An Introductory Approach (sc)
Marc H. Hollender & Charles V. Ford
0-7657-0261-4, $25.00

"Hollender and Ford have produced the classic text for the beginning therapist. Richly illustrated with clinical material, the book clearly provides guidelines for the development of sound ther-apeutic techniques. Although the main thrust is on long-term, insight-oriented therapy, other topics include time-limited therapy, supportive therapy, and psychotherapy combined with pharmacotherapy. Common problem situations and various types of difficult patients are also discussed. This book should be required reading."

—Daniel K. Winstead

TALKING WITH PATIENTS:
A Self Psychological View
Sanford Shapiro
1-56821-598-3, $40.00

"In *Talking with Patients*, Sanford Shapiro provides an eminently practical and user-friendly guide to the clinical application of contemporary psychoanalytic frameworks, including self psychology, control mastery theory, and the intersubjective viewpoint. Therapists at all levels of experience will appreciate and profit from this richly illustrated, down-to-earth text."

—Robert D. Stolorow

**LOVE AND HATE IN THE
ANALYTIC SETTING** (sc)
Glen O. Gabbard
0-7657-0291-6, $40.00

"This book establishes Glen Gabbard as the leading authority on the containment, management, and interpretation of experiences of intense love, pathological erotization, and hate in the transference-countertransference. Gabbard is without peer in his capacity to provide an undogmatic framework of ideas and a body of vivid clinical material with which the analytic clinician might productively navigate the treacherous waters of intense transference and countertransference love, hate, and sexualization."

—Thomas H. Ogden

THE PSYCHOTHERAPIST AS HEALER
T. Byram Karasu
0-7657-0302-5, $45.00

Dr. Karasu's voice transcends the usual boundaries of the profession as he introduces to all therapists—of different disciplines, backgrounds, allegiances, specialties, and areas of expertise—a broader, more universal view of healing psychic pain. Using verbatim clinical exchanges, he reveals his own internal dialogue (including the interpretations he might have made), considers what varied experts have said on the subject, and intervenes with an astonishingly creative and original voice.

**BROKEN STRUCTURES:
Severe Personality Disorders
and Their Treatment** (sc)
Salman Akhtar
0-7657-0255-X, $50.00

"Dr. Akhtar brings to bear a lifetime of study of the classic papers from the past and present, rigorous methodology and scholarship, intellectual honesty, and a keen synthetic mind that weaves the many strands of identity disturbances throughout the severe personality disorders.

"This encyclopedic text is most impressive in its ability to organize all the personality disorders in a modern dimensional system while still retaining the nosological categories that emphasize the centrality of identity disturbances and splitting for the more severe forms. Utilizing his wide net of past and present papers and a clear and very readable style, Akhtar has combined the descriptive and dynamic without sacrificing depth of conceptualization for clarity. A wonderful work."

—Melvin Singer

**BEHAVIORAL
MANAGEMENT GUIDE:
Essential Treatment Strategies
for Adult Psychotherapy**
Muriel Prince Warren
0-7657-0300-9, $125.00   includes CD-ROM
"Behavorial Mangement Guide is the long-awaited exhaustive clinician's resource book for all who daily wend their way through the labyrinths of managed care as well as through limited insurance and clinical treatment settings. This guidebook provides a full *DSM* array of essential diagnostic procedures, concise treatment plans, and

effective treatment aids—all in plain-language behavioral objectives, goals, and interventions. It provides user-friendly outlines, graphs, and tables to make interviewing, charting, case conferencing, and reporting easier, quicker, more case-specific, and remarkably thorough. Dr. Muriel Prince Warren has provided a computer disk to accompany her brilliant clinical enterprise in order to further aid and expedite the processes of documenting, reporting, thinking through, and providing appropriate care to today's managed care and clinic patients. This essential volume will sit on your desk shelf next to your *DSM* and will prove to be of extreme usefulness, interest, and importance!"

—Lawrence E. Hedges

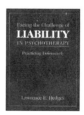

**FACING THE CHALLENGE OF
LIABILITY IN PSYCHOTHERAPY:
Practicing Defensively**
Lawrence E. Hedges
0-7657-0290-8, $112.50   includes CD-ROM
"This is an outstandingly comprehensive and comprehensible handbook about the art of practicing defensively. Before I was even

halfway through this book, I was already making changes in the way I conduct my practice. A real page-turner, this essential guide is a must-read for all practitioners interested in learning about what they must do in order to minimize their chances of having either a complaint or a lawsuit filed against them. Ultimately, however, because it gives clinicians the tools necessary to avoid what might otherwise turn into a ghastly nightmare, perhaps the worst experience in their professional lives, Hedges's book on practicing defensively empowers and holds out hope for all of us."

—Martha Stark

**UNDERSTANDING THE
BORDERLINE MOTHER:
Helping Her Children
Transcend the Intense,
Unpredictable, and
Volatile Relationship**
Christine Ann Lawson
0-7657-0288-6, $45.00

"This interesting, complex book is replete with perceptive insights about the dynamics and behavior of the borderline mother and the

devastating impact that she has on her offspring. I learned a great deal from reading this compelling book."

—Cheryl Glickauf-Hughes

**SELF-INJURY:
Psychotherapy with People
Who Engage in
Self-Inflicted Violence**
Robin E. Connors
0-7657-0264-9, $50.00

"Within the context of safety provided by a therapist who dares to bring her authentic self into the room, the patient is helped to move toward resolution, integration, and wholeness. Connors' book is at once life affirming, heart-warming, and inspiring—a must-read for any of us working with patients who inflict injury upon themselves as a frantic call for help."   —Martha Stark

THE PHOENIX PHENOMENON: Rising from the Ashes of Grief
Joanne T. Jozefowski
0-7657-0209-6, $40.00

"This is an inspirational book for psychotherapists, physicians, clergy, and all of us who must learn to keep living when someone we love has died. Dr. Jozefowski teaches us that grief is not about letting go but making contact: with our loved one, emotions, self, community, values, and hopes. She and her patients show us that these connections can be transforming and, like the Phoenix, can permit one of our saddest moments to become an occasion for rebirth."

—Nicholas A. Covino

MODES OF THERAPEUTIC ACTION: Enhancement of Knowledge, Provision of Experience, and Engagement in Relationship (sc)
Martha Stark
0-7657-0250-9, $40.00

"With *Modes of Therapeutic Action*, Martha Stark has taken the fledgling field of comparative psychoanalysis into a new and important domain. She develops in great detail a framework for contrasting and exploring the major contemporary models of the analytic process. She takes us underneath the slogans and banners of the various schools so that we may compare their underlying concepts and presuppositions. And she demonstrates what different technical systems actually look like in live action by presenting a remarkably rich array of clinical examples. This book will contribute to the enrichment of both the thinking and clinical sensibility of clinicians at all levels of experience and sophistication."

—Stephen A. Mitchell

**THE LANGUAGE
OF PERVERSION AND
THE LANGUAGE OF LOVE** (sc)
Sheldon Bach
0-7657-0230-4, $40.00

"In this clinically important work, Bach shows us a new way of listening and responding to difficult, perverse, and borderline patients. We must go beyond mere mirroring, Bach asserts, and respond in a way that indicates that the patients' words have been heard, understood, and processed so that even disavowed portions of what was said are brought into the discourse and enriched by the dialogue. Yet *The Language of Perversion and the Language of Love* transcends its immediate focus on psychopathology, on sexual and character perversion, to offer a creative and original perspective on the nature of object relations, the nature of the mind, and the human condition."

—Arnold D. Richards &
Arlene Kramer Richards

**BORDERLINE
CONDITIONS AND
PATHOLOGICAL
NARCISSISM** (Lam)
Otto Kernberg
0-87668-762-1, $50.00

"Kernberg delineates the developmental issues that distinguish psychotic, borderline, and narcissistic patients. He then describes the treatment implications that follow from these formulations. He reminds us constantly that object relations include relationships with outside objects as well as their intrapsychic representations. This book will be used as one of the basic texts by clinicians and theoreticians who struggle to master an intellectual and emotional understanding of these difficult patients."

—Gerald Adler

**STRESS RESPONSE
SYNDROMES:
Fourth Edition**
Mardi Horowitz
0-7657-0313-0, $50.00

This book presents the most recent advances in the understanding and treatment of stress response syndromes (posttraumatic stress disorder, grief, and adjustment disorders). For more than twenty years, Dr. Mardi Horowitz has set the standard for psychotherapy with victims of trauma. In this volume, he incorporates the latest research findings into the most comprehensive manual for treatment of stress response syndromes to date. Of invaluable aid to clinicians, this book offers an astute and empathetic understanding of the impact of traumatic events in patients' lives.

**THE BAD OBJECT:
Handling the Negative
Therapeutic Reaction in
Psychotherapy** (sc)
Jeffrey Seinfeld
1-56821-002-7, $50.00

"*The Bad Object* is an exciting and stimulating book. Its author clearly shows a grasp of the theory, but even more important, he demonstrates clinical sensitivity in integrating theory and practice. The book deals with issues throughout treatment and is especially useful for clinicians working with seriously disturbed individuals (i.e., borderline and narcissistic patients). Seinfeld describes difficult patients who could easily be treated as management rather than as therapy cases. It is one of the positive features of this book that allows some therapeutic optimism with these clients. Not many works deal with the theory of analytic treatment and do it well. The clinical chapters alone are worth the price. This book is a major contribution to the field and should be taken seriously by analytically oriented clinicians."

—Eli Leiter

For more information: www.aronson.com

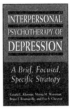

SPLIT SELF/SPLIT OBJECT:
Understanding and Treating
Borderline, Narcissistic, and
Schizoid Disorders (sc)
Philip Manfield
0-7657-0297-5, $40.00

"Dr. Manfield has written a superb book concerning the treatment of the personality disorders. He points out that these patients speak their own language and he provides a clear and beautiful translation of it. His approach blends empathic attunement and a sound understanding of the dynamics of the personality disorders. One of the special features of this volume is that Dr. Manfield takes the reader along in his thinking process, illustrating why he selects one intervention over others. *Split Self/Split Object* is a brilliant and highly readable book."

—Jeffrey Seinfeld

INTERPERSONAL
PSYCHOTHERAPY
OF DEPRESSION:
A Brief, Focused,
Specific Strategy (sc)
Gerald L. Klerman, Myrna M.
Weissman, Bruce J. Rounsaville
and Eve. S. Chevron
1-56821-350-6, $40.00

"The authors—pioneers in the development of a brief, focused, specific strategy of psychotherapy for the treatment of depression— have described their treatment with the precision and clarity that allow others to replicate their methods and evaluate their results. This book marks a major step in the transformation of psychotherapy from a field of competing traditions to a science in which hypotheses can be tested and accepted or rejected. For the first time we will be able to stop arguing about treasured beliefs and start building new treatments based upon the proven results of older ones."

—Robert Michels

**THE PSYCHOLOGY
OF SUICIDE:
A Clinician's Guide to
Evaluation and Treatment**
*Edwin Shneidman, Norman L.
Farberow, & Robert E. Litman*
1-56821-057-4, $45.00

"The range of this volume is enormous. The practical items are all here, but so are the theoretical. It is the most definitive book on suicide to be found."

—Sidney Cohen

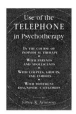

**USE OF THE TELEPHONE
IN PSYCHOTHERAPY**
Joyce K. Aronson, editor
0-7657-0268-1, $50.00

"Here it is! The admission that psychotherapy is done on the telephone. The decision to meet a patient's need for telephone contact is no longer considered a sin of gratification. Rather, this book demonstrates the usefulness of telephone contact in many circumstances, including geographical moves, hospitalization, business travel, crises of aloneness, suicidality, fear of intimacy, and addictions. Abundant clinical examples and a self-preservative chapter on legal and ethical issues further enrich this timely book."

—Jill Scharff

**ATTACHMENT AND
ADULT PSYCHOTHERAPY**
Pat Sable
0-7657-0284-3, $50.00

"Despite its huge influence within psychology and child development, attachment theory has made slow inroads in the world of psychotherapy with adults. One of Bowlby's early American collaborators, Pat Sable has been working in this field for thirty years, and has at last produced the book her friends and colleagues have been waiting for. Sable is the perfect Bowlbian: her calm, trustworthy, unpretentious yet scholarly voice comes through in every page of this immensely readable, indeed unputdownable volume."

—Jeremy Holmes

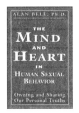

**THE MIND AND HEART IN
HUMAN SEXUAL BEHAVIOR:
Owning and Sharing Our
Personal Truths**
Alan Bell
0-7657-0135-9, $40.00

"Alan Bell is one of the world's foremost authorities on sexual behavior and the psychology of interpersonal relationships. His book, a must-read for anyone interested in the meanings and subtle nuances of human sexuality, is notable for its refreshingly original insights and practically crafted suggestions."

—Robert C. Kolodny

**MEN WITH SEXUAL PROBLEMS
AND WHAT WOMEN CAN DO
TO HELP THEM** (sc)
Eva Margolies
0-7657-0317-3, $25.00

With sensitivity and good sense, Eva Margolies provides a compre-hensive look at how women can help men overcome sexual dys-function. This important book addresses the full range of prob-lems, from premature ejaculation, loss of desire, and impotence to fetishism and sexual addiction. It shows how women can demon-strate understanding of troubled men and gives specific advice on what to say and do to help deal with these problems. A wonder-fully balanced examination of the Viagra revolution completes the book.

**THE PSYCHOPATHIC MIND:
Origins, Dynamics,
and Treatment** (sc)
J. Reid Meloy
0-87668-311-1, $45.00

"This is a superb presentation of what is currently known about the psychopathic personality and its functioning. The discussion is comprehensive and clearly and forcefully articulated, making it maximally useful for clinical and forensic settings. The book would be highly useful and helpful for all clinicians engaged in the evalua-tion and treatment of criminal psychopaths. This extremely important work fills a vacuum in the understanding of psychopathic disorders from the psychological and psychodynamic perspective."

—William W. Meissner

STRAIGHT TALK
ABOUT CRIMINALS:
Understanding and Treating
Antisocial Individuals
Stanton E. Samenow
1-56821-875-3, $40.00

"Dr. Samenow knows more about the criminal personality than anyone I know. The *Straight Talk about Criminals* he gives us, after spending more than twenty-seven years interviewing, evaluating, and treating men, women, and children convicted of a variety of crimes, is a must-read for anyone working with convicted felons as well as for the lay person with questions about the criminal personality and how it got to be that way." —John Douglas

Selected Resources in
Psychotherapy

Cognitive Therapy

Cognitive-Behavioral Treatment for Adult Survivors of Childhood Trauma: Imagery Rescripting *M.R. Smucker & C.V. Dancu* (0-7657-0213-4) $40.00

Cognitive-Behavioral Treatment of Depression *J.S. Klosko & W.C. Sanderson* (0-7657-0152-9) $40.00

Cognitive Therapy: Basic Principles and Applications *R. Leahy* (1-56821-850-8) $50.00

Enhancing Psychodynamic Therapy with Cognitive Behavioral Techniques *T.B. Northcut & N.R. Heller* (0-7657-0181-2) $50.00

Handbook of the Treatment of Anxiety Disorders *C. Lindemann* (1-56821-805-5) $65.00

Interpersonal Process in Cognitive Therapy *J. Safran & Z. Segal* (1-56821-858-3) $50.00 sc

Overcoming Shyness and Social Phobia *R. Rapee* (0-7657-0120-0) $25.00 sc

Practicing Cognitive Therapy: A Guide to Interventions *R. Leahy* (1-56821-824-9) $60.00

Psychosocial Interventions in HIV Disease: A Stage-Focused and Culture-Specific Approach *I. Crawford & B. Fishman* (1-56821-825-7) $40.00 sc

Social Phobia: Clinical Application of Evidence-Based Psychotherapy *R. Rapee & W.C. Sanderson* (0-7657-0004-2) $35.00

Specific Phobias: Clinical Applications of Evidence-Based Psychotherapy *T.J. Bruce & W.C. Sanderson* (1-56821-883-4) $40.00

Treatment of Obsessive-Compulsive Disorder *L.K. McGinn & W.C. Sanderson* (0-7657-0211-8) $40.00

Widening the Scope of Cognitive Therapy: The Therapeutic Relationship, Emotion, and the Process of Change *J. Safran* (0-7657-0138-3) $50.00

Depression

Depressive States & Their Treatment *V. Volkan* (1-56821-223-2) $60.00 sc

Interpersonal Psychotherapy of Depression: A Brief, Focused, Specific Strategy *G.L. Klerman, M.M. Weissman, B.J. Rounsaville, & E.S. Chevron* (1-56821-350-6) $40.00

Psychodynamic Understanding of Depression *W. Gaylin* (1-56821-432-4) $50.00 sc

The Transmission of Depression in Families and Children *G.P. Sholevar* (1-56821-088-4) $50.00

Eating Disorders

Conversations with Anorexics: A Compassionate and Hopeful Journey through the Therapeutic Process *H. Bruch* (1-56821-261-5) $30.00

Psychodynamic Technique in the Treatment of the Eating Disorders *C. Wilson, et al.* (0-87668-622-6) $60.00

Self-Starvation *M. Palazzoli* (1-56821-822-2) $50.00 sc

Starving to Death in a Sea of Objects: The Anorexia Nervosa Syndrome *J. Sours* (0-87668-435-5) $40.00 sc

Existential Psychotherapy

Being-In, Being-For, Being-With *C. Moustakas* (1-56821-537-1) $50.00

Existence *R. May* (1-56821-271-2) $40.00 sc

Existential Family Therapy: Using the Concepts of Viktor Frankl *J. Lantz* (0-87668-578-5) $45.00

Existential Psychotherapy & the Interpretation of Dreams *C. Moustakas* (1-56821-180-5) $45.00

Freud & Freud Therapy

Freud's Technique Papers: A
Contemporary Perspective *S. Ellman*
(0-87668-619-6) $60.00

How Freud Worked *P. Roazen*
(1-56821-556-8) $40.00

The Modern Freudians: Contemporary
Psychoanalytic Technique *C. Ellman et al.*
(0-7657-0229-0) $40.00 sc

On Freud's Couch: Seven New
Interpretations of Freud's Case Histories
I. Matthis & I. Szecsödy
(0-7657-0115-4) $50.00

The Origins of Self and Identity:
Living and Dying in Freud's Psychoanalysis
J.A. Friedman (0-7657-0154-5) $40.00

Gay and Lesbian Issues

**Affirmative Dynamic Psychotherapy
with Gay Men** *C. Cornett, ed.*
(1-56821-001-9) $50.00

Being Homosexual *R. Isay*
(1-56821-276-3) $35.00

Healing Homosexuality: Case Stories of
Reparative Therapy *J. Nicolosi*
(0-7657-0144-8) $40.00 sc

**Psychoanalysis & Male
Homosexuality** *K. Lewes*
(1-56821-484-7) $50.00

Reclaiming the Authentic Self
C. Cornett (1-56821-395-6) $45.00

Group Therapy

**Art & Technique of Analytic Group
Therapy** *M. Grotjahn*
(1-56821-026-4) $35.00 sc

**The Developing Ego & the Emerging
Self in Group Therapy** *D. Flapan &
G. Fenchel* (0-87668-980-2) $40.00

A First Group Psychotherapy Book
E. Pinney (1-56821-617-3) $40.00 sc

**Group Interventions with Children,
Adolescents, & Parents** *E. Buchholz &
J. Mishne* (1-56821-243-7) $50.00 sc

How to Do Groups *W. Friedman*
(1-56821-117-1) $40.00

**Identity Group Psychotherapy with
Adolescents** *A. Rachman*
(1-56821-658-0) $50.00 sc

Psychoanalytic Group Therapy
K. König & W. Lindner (1-56821-119-8) $40.00

**Resolving Resistance in Group
Psychotherapy** *L. Rosenthal*
(1-56821-193-7) $35.00

Therapists in the Community
M. Dumont (1-56821-405-7) $40.00 sc

Hypnosis

**Handbook of Hypnosis for
Professionals** *R. Udolf*
(1-56821-727-7) $70.00

The New Hypnosis in Sex Therapy:
Cognitive-Behavioral Methods for Clinicians
D. Araoz (0-7657-0137-5) $40.00 sc

Intimacy

Fearful Symmetry: The Development and
Treatment of Sadomasochism *J. Novick &
K. K. Novick* (1-56821-652-1) $45.00

Intimacy and Infidelity: Separation-
Individuation Perspectives *S. Akhtar &
S. Kramer* (1-56821-775-7) $40.00

Mapping the Terrain of the Heart:
Passion, Tenderness, and the Capacity to Love
S. Goldbart & D. Wallin
(1-56821-790-0) $30.00 sc

Mahler

Mahler and Kohut: Perspectives on
Development, Psychopathology, and
Technique *S. Kramer & S. Akhtar*
(1-56821-785-4) $35.00 sc

Mind/Body

Mind–Body Problems: Psychotherapy
with Psychosomatic Disorders *J. S. Finell*
(1-56821-654-8) $70.00

Psychosomatic Symptoms *C.P.Wilson
& I. Mintz, eds.* (0-87668-877-6) $65.00

Narcissism

Disorders of Narcissism: Diagnostic,
Clinical, and Empirical Implications
E.F. Ronningstam (0-7657-0259-2) $35.00

Impact of Narcissism: The Errant
Therapist on a Chaotic Quest *P. Giovacchini*
(0-7657-0234-7) $40.00

The Mask of Shame *L. Wurmser*
(1-56821-406-5) $70.00

Narcissistic Wounds *J. Cooper &
N. Maxwell* (1-56821-747-1) $25.00

Slings & Arrows: Narcissistic Injury & Its
Treatment *J. Levin* (0-87668-550-5) $50.00

**Treatment of the Narcissistic
Neuroses** *H. Spotnitz & P. Meadow*
(1-56821-416-2) $50.00 sc

Object Relations

Body and Soul: The Role of Object
Relations in Faith, Shame, and Healing
H. Bronheim (0-7657-0162-6) $40.00

**Containing Rage, Terror, and
Despair:** An Object Relations Approach to
Psychotherapy *J. Seinfeld*
(1-56821-578-9) $50.00

From Inner Sources: New Directions in
Object Relations Psychotherapy
N. Hamilton, ed. (0-87668-540-8) $45.00

From Instinct to Self: Selected Papers of
W.R.D. Fairbairn (Two Vols.) *D. Scharff &
E. Fairbairn Birtles* (1-56821-366-2) $80.00

Internal World, External Reality
O. Kernberg (1-56821-311-5) $50.00 sc

The Matrix of the Mind *T. H. Ogden*
(1-56821-051-5) $40.00 sc

Object Relations Brief Therapy: The
Therapeutic Relationship in Short-Term Work
M. Stadter (1-56821-660-2) $60.00

Object Relations Couple Therapy
D. E. Scharff, & J. S. Scharff
(1-56821-436-7) $50.00 sc

**Object Relations and the Developing
Ego in Therapy** *A. Horner*
(1-56821-708-0) $50.00 sc

Object Relations: A Dynamic Bridge
Between Individual & Family Treatment
S. Slipp (0-87668-527-0) $40.00 sc

Object Relations Family Therapy
J. S. Scharff & D.E. Scharff
(0-87668-517-3) $60.00 sc

Object Relations Individual Therapy
J.S. Scharff & D.E. Scharff
(0-7657-0117-0) $70.00

Object Relations Psychotherapy:
An Individualized and Interactive Approach to
Diagnosis and Treatment *C. Glickauf-Hughes*
(0-7657-0069-7) $55.00

**Object Relations Theory and
Practice:** An Introduction *D.E. Scharff*
(1-56821-419-7) $60.00

Personal Relations Therapy: The
Collected Papers of H.J.S. Guntrip *J. Hazel,
ed.* (1-56821-164-3) $60.00

Primacy of Structure: Psychotherapy of
Underlying Character Pathology *A. Horner*
(0-87668-748-6) $55.00

A Primer of Object Relations
J.S . Scharff & D.E. Scharff
(1-56821-774-9) $30.00 sc

The Primitive Edge of Experience
T.H. Ogden (0-87668-290-5) $40.00 sc

**Projective & Introjective
Identification and the Use of the
Therapist's Self** *J.S. Scharff*
(0-87668-530-0) $50.00

**Projective Identification and
Psychotherapeutic Technique**
T.H. Ogden (0-87668-542-4) $40.00 sc

**Psychoanalytic Object Relations
Therapy** *A. Horner* (1-56821-637-8) $40.00

**Refinding the Object & Reclaiming
the Self** *D.E. Scharff* (0-87668-458-4)
$60.00

Regression to Dependence
R. Van Sweden (1-56821-279-8) $45.00

**The Self and the Ego in
Psychotherapy** *N.G. Hamilton*
(1-56821-659-9) $40.00

Self and Others: Object Relations Theory
in Practice *N.G. Hamilton*
(0-87668-544-0) $40.00 sc

The Sexual Relationship: An Object
Relations View of Sex and the Family
D.E. Scharff (0-7657-0165-0) $50.00 sc

Subjects of Analysis *T.H. Ogden*
(1-56821-803-6) $40.00 sc

**Vision & Separation Between Mother
& Baby** *K. Wright* (0-87668-559-9) $60.00

Pastoral Counseling

Parish Counseling *E. Jackson*
(0-87668-672-2) $40.00

Pastor & Patient *R. Dayringer*
(1-56821-512-6) $45.00 sc

**Psychological Perspectives on
Traditional Jewish Practices**
S. Linke (0-7657-6036-3) $30.00

**Psychotherapy of the Religious
Patient** *M. Spero* (1-56821-811-7) $50.00 sc

Transference & Transcendence
D. Liechty (1-56821-434-0) $45.00

Professional Concerns

**Dealing with the Therapist's
Vulnerability to Depression**
S. Heath (0-87668-612-9) $40.00

The New Informants: The Betrayal of
Confidentiality in Psychoanalysis &
Psychotherapy *C. Bollas & D. Sundelson*
(1-56821-595-9) $35.00

On Being a Psychotherapist
C. Goldberg (1-56821-163-5) $50.00 sc

Psychoanalysis: The Impossible Profession
J. Malcolm (1-56821-342-5) $30.00

Psychodynamic Supervision:
Perspectives of the Supervisor and the
Supervisee *M. Rock*
(1-56821-693-9) $50.00 sc

The Psychotherapist: Use and Abuse of
Psychological Influence *G. Warme*
(1-56821-736-6) $50.00 sc

Psychotherapy with Psychotherapists
F. Kaslow (1-56821-326-3) $45.00 sc

Therapists at Risk: Perils of the Intimacy
of the Therapeutic Relationship *L. Hedges, et
al.* (1-56821-827-3) $50.00

**Training and Teaching the Mental
Health Professional:** An In-Depth
Approach *J. Yalof* (1-56821-710-2) $50.00 sc

**What Therapists Learn About
Themselves and How They Learn It**
E. Messner, et al. (1-56821-188-0) $40.00 sc

Psychiatry

**Dynamic Therapy in Brief
Hospitalization** *J. Oldham &
M. Russakoff* (0-87668-965-9) $40.00

The History of Psychiatry *F. Alexander
& S. Selesnick* (1-56821-754-4) $60.00 sc

Psychoanalysis

Analysts at Work *J. Reppen*
(1-56821-423-5) $50.00 sc

The Art of Unknowing *S. Kurtz*
(0-87668-860-1) $45.00

The Autonomous Self: The Work of John D. Sutherland *J.S. Scharff, ed.* (1-56821-008-6) $65.00

The Bad Object *J. Seinfeld* (1-56821-002-7) $50.00 sc

The Bipersonal Field *R. Langs* (0-87668-246-8) $50.00

Classics in Psychoanalytic Technique *R. Langs* (0-87668-744-3) $95.00

Clinical Psychoanalysis *S. Orgel & B. Fine, eds.* (0-87668-368-5) $60.00

Clinical & Social Realities *D. Kaplan* (1-56821-472-3) $50.00

The Collected Papers of David Rapaport *M. Gill* (1-56821-473-1) $95.00

The Common Ground of Psychoanalysis *R. Wallerstein* (0-87668-555-6) $60.00

Consciousness Redux: Waking, Sleeping, Dreaming, and States In Between *M. Stein & B. Stimmel* (0-7657-0119-7) $60.00

Countertransference and Regression *L.B. Boyer* (1-56821-706-4) $40.00

Cultivating Freud's Garden in France *M. Michel Oliner* (0-87668-995-0) $60.00

Danger & Defense: The Technique of Close Process Attention *M. Goldberger* (1-56821-583-5) $65.00

The Death of Psychoanalysis: Murder? Suicide? or Rumor Greatly Exaggerated? *R.M. Prince* (0-7657-0147-2) $50.00

Deepening the Treatment *J.S. Hall* (0-7657-017-66) $40.00

Dialogue with Erik Erikson *R. Evans* (1-56821-561-4) $35.00 sc

Difficulties in the Analytic Encounter *J. Klauber* (0-87668-430-4) $40.00

Diverse Techniques of Analysis by 27 Eminent Clinicians *B. Wolman* (1-56821-493-6) $60.00 sc

Dynamics of Development & the Therapeutic Process *R. Lasky* (0-87668-565-3) $60.00

The Ego & Analysis of Defense *P. Gray* (1-56821-192-9) $50.00

The Ego at the Center of Clinical Technique *F. Busch* (1-56821-471-5) $50.00

The Electrified Tightrope *M. Eigen* (0-87668-294-8) $50.00

Encounters with Autistic States *T. Mitrani & J. Mitrani* (0-7657-0066-2) $50.00

Envy *H. Boris* (1-56821-083-3) $40.00

Foundations of Psychopathology *J. Nemiah* (0-87668-100-3) $40.00

A Framework for the Imaginary *J. Mitrani* (1-56821-479-0) $45.00

The Freedom to Inquire: Self Psychological Perspectives on Women's Issues, Masochism, & the Therapeutic Relationship *E. Menaker* (1-56821-475-8) $50.00

God is a Woman *R. Lopéz-Corvo* (1-56821-862-1) $40.00

Great Cases in Psychoanalysis *H. Greenwald, ed.* (0-87668-786-9) $45.00

Heresy: Sandor Rado & the Psychoanalytic Movement *P. Roazen & B. Swerdloff* (1-56821-321-2) $50.00 sc

Inner Torment: Living Between Conflict and Fragmentation *S. Akhtar* (0-7657-0159-6) $45.00

Introduction to Contemporary Psychoanalysis *A. Bernstein & G. Warner* (0-87668-303-0) $40.00 sc

The Joy of Suffering: Psychoanalytic Theory & Therapy of Masochism *S. Panken* (1-56821-120-1) $40.00 (0-87668-065-1) $35.00 sc

Knowledge & Authority in the Psychoanalytic Relationship *O. Renik* (0-7657-0139-1) $40.00 sc

---

The Language of Perversion and the Language of Love *S. Bach*
(0-7657-0230-4) $40.00 sc

Love and Attachment: Contemporary Issues and Treatment Consideration *C. Tosone & T. Aiello, eds.* (0-7657-0185-5) $40.00

The Many Faces of Deceit *H.K. Gediman & J.S. Lieberman*
(1-56821-592-4) $45.00

Melanie Klein *P. Grosskurth*
(1-56821-445-6) $50.00

Melting the Darkness: The Dyad and Principles of Clinical Practice *W. Poland*
(1-56821-816-8) $45.00

Modern Psychoanalysis of the Schizophrenic Patient *H. Spotnitz*
(0-7657-0157-X) $50.00 sc

New Introduction to the Work of Bion *L. Grinberg, et al.*
(0-87668-440-1) $40.00 sc

Obsessional Neuroses: Developmental Psychopathology *H. Nagera*
(1-56821-151-1) $40.00 sc

Omnipotent Fantasies and the Vulnerable Self *C. Ellman & J. Reppen*
(0-7657-0046-8) $50.00

Phantasy in Everyday Life *J. Segal*
(1-56821-753-6) $45.00 sc

The Power of Countertransference: Innovations in Analytic Technique *K.J. Maroda* (1-56821-431-6) $35.00 sc

The Practice of Psychoanalytic Therapy *K. König*
(1-56821-353-0) $50.00 sc

A Prophetic Analyst: Erich Fromm's Contribution to Psychoanalysis *M. Cortina & M. Maccoby* (1-56821-621-1) $50.00

Psychoanalysis & Catholicism *B. Wolman* (1-56821-715-3) $40.00 sc

Psychic Deadness *M. Eigen*
(1-56821-735-8) $50.00

A Psychoanalyst Explores the Alternate Therapies *S. Appelbaum*
(1-56821-168-6) $50.00 sc

The Psychoanalytic Process: A Case Illustration *P. Dewald*
(1-56821-194-5) $50.00 sc

The Psychoanalytic Understanding of the Dream *P. Sloane*
(0-87668-362-6) $40.00

Psychoanalysis & Psychopathology *P. Holzman* (1-56821-588-6) $45.00

The Psychotherapeutic Instrument *S. Olinick* (0-87668-403-7) $40.00

The Psychotic Core *M. Eigen*
(0-87668-153-4) $50.00 sc

Reaching the Affect *E. F. Hammer*
(0-87668-818-0) $50.00

Reluctant Treasures *G. Warme*
(1-56821-217-8) $50.00

Reparation *H. Clegg*
(1-56821-557-6) $45.00 sc

Rethinking Clinical Technique *F. Busch* (0-7657-0183-9) $40.00

Reverie & Interpretation: Sensing Something Human *T.H. Ogden*
(0-7657-0076-X) $40.00
(0-7657-0249-5) $30.00 sc

The Seasons of Life: Separation-Individuation Perspectives *S. Akhtar & S. Kramer, eds.* (0-7657-0055-7) $45.00

Semrad: Heart of a Therapist *S. Rako & H. Mazer, eds.* (0-87668-684-6) $40.00

Sleights of Mind *H. Boris*
(1-56821-082-5) $60.00

Spleen and Nostalgia: A Life and Work in Psychoanalysis *J.Gedo* (0-7657–0082-4) $40.00

Tactics & Techniques in Psychoanalytic Therapy: Vol. I *P.L. Giovacchini* (1-56821-110-4) $60.00 sc

---

For more information: www.aronson.com

**Tactics & Techniques in
Psychoanalytic Therapy: Vol. III**
P.L. Giovacchini (0-87668-789-3) $55.00

**Techniques of Working with
Resistance** *D. Millman & G. Goldman*
(0-87668-616-1) $60.00

**The Therapeutic Experience and
Its Setting:** A Clinical Dialogue *R. Langs &
L. Stone* (0-87668-405-3) $50.00

**Unconscious Communication in
Everyday Life** *R. Langs*
(1-56821-106-6) $40.00 sc

Use of Interpretation in Treatment:
Technique and Art *E. Hammer, ed.*
(1-56821-111-2) $50.00

**What Do You Get When You Cross a
Dandelion with a Rose?:** The True Story
of Psychoanalysis *V. Volkan*
(0-87668-638-2) $45.00

**What is Effective in Psychoanalytic
Therapy** *W. Meissner*
(0-87668-572-6) $40.00

The Work of Hanna Segal *H. Segal*
(0-87668-422-3) $50.00

The Work of Hans Loewald
G. Fogel, ed. (0-87668-615-3) $50.00

Working in Depth: A Clinician's Guide to
Framework and Flexibility in the Analytic
Relationship *E. Adler & J.L. Bachant*
(0-7657-0160-X) $60.00

Psychopharmacology

**Handbook of Clinical
Psychopharmacology** *J. Tupin, et al.*
(0-87668-523-8) $60.00

Psychotherapy & Medication: A
Dynamic Integration *M. Schachter*
(0-87668-296-4) $65.00

The Sovereign Self: Toward a
Phenomenology of Self Experience
F. von Broembsen (0-7657-0164-2) $50.00

Psychotherapy

Acting Out *L. Abt & S. Weissman*
(1-56821-778-1) $50.00 sc

Active Psychotherapy *H. Greenwald*
(0-87668-663-3) $50.00

The Art of Hating *G. Schoenewolf*
(0-87668-693-5) $40.00

**The Art of Intervention in Dynamic
Psychotherapy** *B. Kaplan*
(0-87668-983-7) $50.00

Balancing Empathy & Interpretation
L. Josephs (1-56821-447-2) $60.00

**Basic Techniques of Psychodynamic
Psychotherapy** *M. Nichols &
T. Paolino, Jr.* (1-56821-618-1) $50.00

Beyond Technique: An Individualized
Approach to Psychotherapy *L. LeShan*
(1-56821-550-9) $40.00

Bridges of Compassion: Insights and
Interventions in Developmental Disabilities
A. Campbell & L. Ladner
(0-7657-0131-6) $35.00

**Brief Strategic Solution-Oriented
Therapy of Phobic and Obsessive
Disorders** *G. Nardone*
(1-56821-804-4) $45.00

**Building a Neuropsychology
Practice:** A Guide to Respecialization *M.H.
Podd & D.P. Seelig* (0-7657-0146-4) $40.00

The Chambers of Memory: PTSD in the
Life Stories of U.S. Vietnam Veterans
H.W. Chalsma (1-56821-691-2) $40.00

Character and Self-Experience:
Working with Obsessive-Compulsive,
Depressive-Masochistic, Narcissistic, and
Other Character Styles *L. Josephs*
(1-56821-580-0) $40.00 sc

Clinical Uses of Drawings *G. Oster &
S. Montgomery* (1-56821-199-6) $50.00

For more information: www.aronson.com

Compassion: The Core Value that Animates Psychotherapy *R. Lewin* (1-56821-678-5) $50.00

Constructing Therapeutic Narratives *H. Omer & N. Alon* (1-56821-856-7) $50.00

Conversations in Psychotherapy *R. V. Fitzgerald* (0-87668-561-0) $50.00

Coping with Anxiety: Integrated Approaches to Treatment *W.W. Menninger* (1-56821-788-9) $20.00

Cotherapy with Individuals, Families, & Groups *S. Hoffman, S. Gafni, & B. Laub* (1-56821-316-6) $35.00 sc

Creative Collaboration in Psychotherapy: Making Room for Life *R. Lewin* (0-7657-0075-1) $35.00

Crisis Intervention *E. Lindemann* (1-56821-468-5) $50.00 sc

Cultivating Intuition *P. Lomas* (0-87668-528-9) $40.00

Cultural Psychotherapy: Working with Culture in the Clinical Encounter *K.M. Seeley* (0-7657-0224-X) $40.00

Culture and Therapy: An Integrative Approach *J. Fish* (1-56821-545-2) $50.00

Curative Factors in Dynamic Psychotherapy *S. Slipp* (1-56821-097-3) $50.00 sc

Deconstruction of Psychotherapy *T.B. Karasu* (1-56821-821-4) $40.00 sc

Developmental Conflicts and Diagnostic Evaluation in Adolescent Psychotherapy *R.A. Gardner* (0-7657-0206-1) $30.00 sc

Dialogue Concerning Contemporary Psychodynamic Therapy *R. Chessick* (1-56821-371-9) $30.00 sc

Dirty Words: The Expressive Power of Taboo *A. Arango* (1-56821-799-4) $40.00 sc

Don't Lose Your Patients!: Responding to Clients Who Want to Quit Treatment *H.S. Strean* (0-7657-0171-5) $40.00

The Dually Diagnosed: A Therapist's Guide to Helping the Substance Abusing, Psychologically Disturbed Patient *D. Ortman* (1-56821-770-6) $40.00

Dynamic Therapy of the Older Patient *W. Myers* (0-87668-623-4) $45.00

Effecting Change in Psychotherapy *S. Appelbaum* (1-56821-600-9) $45.00 sc

Enactment: Toward a New Approach to the Therapeutic Relationship *S.J. Ellman & M. Moskowitz* (1-56821-584-3) $50.00

The Encyclopedia of Evolving Technique in Psychodynamic Psychotherapy *I. Solomon* (0-87668-511-4) $60.00

Faces in a Cloud: Intersubjectivity in Personality Theory *G. Atwood & R. Stolorow* (0-7657-0200-2) $30.00 sc

Fear of Humiliation: Integrated Treatment of Social Phobia and Comorbid Conditions *W.W. Menninger* (1-56821-465-0) $25.00 sc

The First Encounter: The Beginnings in Psychotherapy *W.A. Console, et al.* (1-56821-141-4) $50.00 sc

Gaslighting, the Double Whammy, Interrogation, and Other Methods of Covert Control in Psychotherapy & Analysis *T. Dorpat* (1-56821-828-1) $50.00

Getting Started *J. Kotin* (1-56821-451-0) $50.00

Great Ideas in Psychotherapy *R. Chessick* (0-87668-787-7) $60.00

The Handbook of Problem-Oriented Psychotherapy: A Guide for Psychologists, Social Workers, Psychiatrists, and Other Mental Health Professionals *A. H. Chapman & M. Chapman-Santana* (1-56821-682-3) $40.00

The History of Psychotherapy
J. Ehrenwald, ed. (0-87668-280-8) $55.00

How Can Talking Help? An Introduction
to the Technique of Analytic Therapy
R. Mendelsohn (0-87668-503-3) $50.00

How Psychotherapy Heals
R. Chessick (0-87668-821-0) $45.00

**How to Use Computers and
Cyberspace in the Clinical Practice
of Psychotherapy** *J. Fink*
(0-7657-0173-1) $40.00

Humor and Psychotherapy
T. Kuhlman (1-56821-317-4) $25.00 sc

If You Love Me Don't Love Me:
Undoing Reciprocal Double Binds and Other
Methods of Change in Couple and Family
Therapy *M. Elkaïm* (0-7657-0048-4) $30.00 sc

Illusion and Disillusionment:
Core Issues in Psychotherapy *S.H. Teitelbaum*
(0-7657-0219-3) $45.00

**Individual and Group Therapy and
Work with Parents in Adolescent
Psychotherapy** *R.A. Gardner*
(0-7657-0207-X) $25.00 sc

**Image Formation and
Psychotherapy** *M. Horowitz*
(1-56821-730-7) $50.00 sc

**In Search of the Lost Mother of
Infancy** *L. Hedges* (1-56821-274-7) $40.00

**The Infantile Psychotic Self & Its
Fates** *V. Volkan* (1-56821-379-4) $50.00

Interpreting & Holding *J. Seinfeld*
(0-87668-501-7) $50.00

Intricate Engagements: The
Collaborative Basis of Therapeutic Change
S. Frankel (1-56821-590-8) $50.00

**Invitation to Psychodynamic
Psychology** *A. Lemma-Wright*
(1-56821-629-7) $40.00 sc

Jokes: Their Purpose & Meaning *H. Strean*
(1-56821-070-1) $40.00

Leaps: Facing Risks in Offering a
Constructive Therapeutic Response When
Unusual Measures are Necessary
R. Mendelsohn (0-87668-566-1) $55.00

Life After Psychotherapy *T. Davison*
(1-56821-849-4) $30.00

**Listening Perspectives in
Psychotherapy** *L. Hedges*
(0-87668-577-7) $50.00 sc

Losing & Fusing: Borderline Transitional
Object and Self Relations *R. Lewin &
C. Schulz* (0-87668-490-8) $55.00

Love and Hate in the Analytic Setting
G. Gabbard (1-56821-671-8) $40.00

**The Manifest Dream & Its Use in
Therapy** *R. Mendelsohn*
(0-87668-766-4) $50.00

Masochism and the Emergent Ego
E. Menaker (1-56821-837-0) $50.00 sc

Memories of Sexual Betrayal: Truth,
Fantasy, Repression, and Dissociation
R. Gardner (1-56821-704-8) $50.00

Modes of Therapeutic Action:
Enhancement of Knowledge, Provision of
Experience, and Engagement in Relationship
M. Stark (0-7657-0202-9) $60.00

**The Neurobiological and
Developmental Basis for
Psychotherapeutic Intervention**
M. Moskowitz, et al. (0-7657-0097-2) $50.00

**Nuances of Technique in Dynamic
Psychotherapy** *M. Horowitz*
(0-87668-859-8) $50.00

On Psychotherapy *P. Clarkson*
(1-56821-310-7) $45.00 sc

101 Therapeutic Successes
G. Schoenewolf (1-56821-841-9) $45.00 sc

Optimal Responsiveness: How
Therapists Heal Their Patients *H. Bacal, ed.*
(0-7657-0114-6) $55.00

Participant Observation
L. Havens (1-56821-108-2) $30.00 sc

Prevention in Mental Health *H. Parens*
& S. Kramer (1-56821-027-2) $27.50 sc

A Primer of Clinical Intersubjectivity
J. Natterson & R. Friedman
(1-56821-446-4) $35.00 sc

A Primer of Kleinian Therapy
I. Solomon (1-56821-391-3) $45.00 sc

**A Primer on Working with
Resistance** *M. Stark*
(1-56821-093-0) $45.00

Principles of Interpretation: Mastering
Clear and Concise Interventions in
Psychotherapy *S. Levy*
(1-56821-798-6) $45.00 sc

**Psychotherapeutic Intervention in
Hysterical Disorders** *W. Mueller &*
A. Aniskiewicz (0-87668-913-6) $50.00

The Psychotherapist's Interventions:
Integrating Psychodynamic Perspectives in
Clinical Practice *T. B. Karasu*
(1-56821-689-0) $45.00

Psychotherapy: A Basic Text *R. Langs*
(0-87668-466-5) $70.00

Psychotherapy: The Art of Wooing Nature
S. Roth (0-7657-0252-5) $35.00

Psychotherapy: The Analytic Approach
M. Aronson & M. Scharfman
(0-87668-508-4) $60.00

**Psychotherapy of Antisocial
Behavior and Depression in
Adolescence** *R.A. Gardner*
(0-7657-0208-8) $22.00 sc

Psychotherapy for Depression
T.B. Karasu (0-87668-691-9) $40.00

**Psychotherapy of Preoedipal
Conditions** *H. Spotnitz*
(1-56821-633-5) $50.00 sc

**Psychotherapy of the Quiet
Borderline Patient** *V. Sherwood &*
C. Cohen (1-56821-060-4) $50.00

Psychotherapy with the Elderly:
Becoming Methuselah's Echo *G. Bouklas*
(0-7657-0051-4) $60.00

**Psychotherapy with the Orthodox
Jew** *H. Strean* (1-56821-230-5) $40.00

Redecision Therapy: A Brief Action-
Oriented Approach *C. Lennox*
(0-7657-0043-3) $40.00

**Reaching Across Boundaries of
Culture and Class:** Widening the Scope of
Psychotherapy *R. Perez-Foster, M. Moskowitz,*
& R. Javier (1-56821-487-1) $50.00

**Remembering, Repeating & Working
Through Childhood Trauma**
L.E. Hedges (1-56821-228-3) $50.00

Resolving Treatment Impasses: The
Difficult Patient *T. Saretsky*
(0-7657-0095-6) $40.00

Return from Madness *K. Degen &*
E. Nasper (1-56821-625-4) $50.00

Sandor Ferenczi: The Psychotherapist of
Tenderness and Passion *A. W. Rachman*
(1-56821-100-7) $60.00

Second Opinions: Sixty Psychotherapy
Patients Evaluate Their Therapists
L.D. Kassan (0-7657-0205-3) $40.00 sc

Shrink Rap: Sixty Psychotherapists Discuss
Their Work, Their Lives, & the State of Their
Field *L.D. Kassan* (0-7657-0017-4) $50.00

**Specialized Techniques for Specific
Clinical Problems in Psychotherapy**
T.B. Karasu & L. Bellak (1-56821-189-9) $50.00 sc

Split Self/Split Object *P. Manfield*
(0-87668-460-6) $55.00

Successful Psychotherapy: A Caring,
Loving Relationship *C. Patterson & S. Hidore*
(1-56821-795-1) $40.00

Technique & Practice of Intensive Psychotherapy *R. Chessick*
(0-87668-657-9) $60.00

The Technique & Practice of Listening in Intensive Psychotherapy
R. Chessick (0-87668-300-6) $50.00 sc

Technique in Transition *R. Langs*
(0-87668-349-9) $75.00

The Technique of Psychoanalytic Psychotherapy Vol I. *R. Langs*
(0-87668-104-6) $70.00

The Technique of Psychoanalytic Psychotherapy Vol II. *R. Langs*
(0-87668-105-4) $60.00

The Technique of Psychotherapy, Parts One & Two *L. Wolberg*
(1-56821-498-7) $150.00

Terrifying Transferences: Aftershocks of Childhood Trauma *L.E. Hedges*
(0-7657-0225-8) $65.00

Theory & Therapy in Dynamic Psychiatry *J. Masserman*
(1-56821-511-8) $50.00 sc

The Therapeutic Dialogue
S. Lal Sharma (1-56821-656-4) $50.00 sc

The Therapeutic Environment
R. Langs (0-87668-385-5) $60.00

Therapeutic Partnership
C. Goldberg (1-56821-325-5) $50.00 sc

The Therapist's Emotional Survival: Dealing with the Pain of Exploring Trauma
S.D. Perlman (0-7657-0175-8) $40.00

The Therapist Is the Therapy: Effective Psychotherapy II *L. Fierman*
(0-7657-0047-6) $45.00 sc

A Thing Apart: Love and Reality in the Therapeutic Relationship *I. Steingart*
(1-56821-304-2) $55.00

The Traumatic Bond Between the Psychotherapist and Managed Care
K. Weisgerber, ed. (0-7657-0180-4) $40.00

Treatment of Emotional Disorders
S. Halleck (0-87668-263-8) $45.00

Treatment of Obsessive and Compulsive Behaviors *L. Salzman*
(1-56821-422-7) $50.00 sc

Turning Points in Analytic Therapy: The Classic Cases *G. Schoenewolf*
(0-87668-819-9) $50.00

Turning Points in Analytic Therapy: From Winnicott to Kernberg *G. Schoenewolf*
(0-87668-809-1) $50.00

Unconscious Fantasy in Psychotherapy *K. Levin*
(0-87668-260-3) $50.00

Understanding & Treating the Psychopath *D. Doren*
(1-56821-791-9) $50.00 sc

The Use of Humor in Psychotherapy
H. Strean (1-56821-084-1) $35.00

Useful Servants: Psychodynamic Approaches to Clinical Practice *S. Levine*
(1-56821-844-3) $40.00

What Constitutes the Patient in Psychotherapy *R. Chessick*
(0-87668-549-1) $45.00

When Nothing Else Works: Innovative Interventions with Intractable Individuals
H. Strean (0-7657-007-43) $40.00 sc

When Things Get Worse *H. Strupp, et al.* (1-56821-372-7) $50.00 sc

Why I Became a Psychotherapist
J. Reppen, ed. (0-7657-0170-7) $50.00

Why Psychotherapists Fail
R. Chessick,. (0-87668-700-1) $40.00

Wit & Wisdom in Dynamic Psychotherapy *G. Bauer*
(0-87668-768-0) $50.00

Working the Organizing Experience
L. Hedges (1-56821-255-0) $60.00

For more information: www.aronson.com

Working with Traits: Psychotherapy of
Personality Disorders *J. Paris*
(0-7657-0096-4) $50.00

Reference Works

A Dictionary for Psychotherapists
R. Chessick (0-87668-338-3) $65.00

Relational Therapy

**Attachment, Intimacy, and
Autonomy:** Using Attachment Theory in
Adult Psychotherapy *J. Holmes*
(1-56851-872-9) $30.00 sc

Close Encounters: A Relational View of
the Therapeutic Process *R. Winer*
(0-87668-165-8) $40.00

Sándor Ferenczi *M. Stanton*
(0-87668-569-6) $45.00

Schizophrenia

**Issues & Controversies in the
Psychotherapy of Schizophrenia**
J. Gunderson & L. Mosher
(1-56821-397-2) $50.00 sc

**Psychotherapeutic Intervention
in Schizophrenia** *L. Hill*
(1-56821-313-1) $40.00 sc

The Psychotherapy of Schizophrenia
J. Strauss, et al. (1-56821-165-1) $50.00 sc

Psychotherapy of Schizophrenia
B. Karon & G. VandenBos
(1-56821-232-1) $60.00 sc

The Psychotic Patient *D. Greenfeld*
(1-56821-343-3) $40.00 sc

Schizophrenia & Civilization
E. Torrey (0-87668-380-4) $40.00

Self Psychology

Empathic Attunement *C. Rowe, Jr. &
D. Mac Isaac* (0-87668-551-3) $40.00 sc

The Intersubjective Perspective
R.D. Stolorow, G.E. Atwood & B. Brandchaft
(1-56821-053-1) $40.00 sc

**Psychology of the Self & the
Treatment of Narcissism**
R. Chessick (0-87668-171-2) $50.00 sc

Talking with Patients: A Self
Psychological View *S. Shapiro*
(1-56821-598-3) $40.00

**Using Self Psychology in
Psychotherapy** *H. Jackson*
(1-56821-044-2) $40.00 sc

Sexuality and Sex Therapy

Female Sexuality: Contemporary
Engagements *D. Bassin*
(0-7657-0081-6) $60.00

Healing Homosexuality: Case Stories of
Reparative Therapy *J. Nicolosi*
(0-7657-0144-8) $40.00 sc

Homosexuality *I. Bieber*
(0-87668-989-6) $50.00

Homosexuality: Psychoanalytic Therapy
C.W. Socarides (0-87668-883-0) $60.00

**The Mind & Heart in Sexual
Behavior:** Owning and Sharing Our
Personal Truths *A.P. Bell*
(0-7657-0135-9) $40.00

The New Hypnosis in Sex Therapy:
Cognitive-Behavioral Methods for Clinicians
D. Araoz (0-7657-0137-5) $40.00 sc

Night Thoughts *A. Offit*
(1-56821-458-8) $25.00 sc

**Reparative Therapy of Male
Homosexuality** *J. Nicolosi*
(0-7657-0142-1) $40.00 sc

**Sexual Animosity Between Men &
Women** *G. Schoenewolf*
(0-87668-933-0) $40.00

The Sexual Self: How Character Shapes
Sexual Experience *A. Offit*
(1-56821-548-7) $25.00

Sexual Unfolding *L. Sarrel & P. Sarrel*
(1-56821-675-0) $50.00 sc

Solving Common Sexual Problems
S. Levine (0-7657-0121-9) $30.00 sc

Treating Sexual Shame: A New Map for
Overcoming Dysfunction, Abuse, and
Addiction *A.S. Hastings* (0-7657-0103-0) $40.00

Treatment of Sexual Dysfunction
W. Hartman & M. Fithian
(1-56821-368-9) $50.00 sc

The Wounded Healer: Addiction-
Sensitive Approach to the Sexually Exploitative
Professional *R. Irons & J.P. Schneider*
(1-56821-763-3) $35.00

Short-Term Therapy

**Basic Principles & Techniques in
Short-Term Psychotherapy**
H. Davanloo, ed. (1-56821-354-9) $50.00 sc

Brief vs. Long Psychotherapy: When,
Why, & How *J. Gustafson*
(1-56821-470-7) $55.00

**A Casebook in Time Limited
Psychotherapy** *J. Mann & R. Goldman*
(1-56821-210-0) $40.00 sc

**The Complex Secret of Brief
Psychotherapy:** A Panorama of Approaches
J. Gustafson (0-7657-0063-8) $50.00 sc

**Crises & Special Problems in
Psychoanalysis & Psychotherapy**
L. Bellak with P. Faithorn
(1-56821-351-4) $45.00 sc

Empathic Brief Psychotherapy
B. Seruya (0-7657-0067-0) $35.00

**Handbook of Short-Term
Therapy Groups** *M. Rosenbaum*
(0-7657-0045-X) $65.00

Short-Term Dynamic Psychotherapy
H. Davanloo, ed. (0-87668-301-4) $60.00 sc

**Treating the Neurotic Patient in Brief
Psychotherapy** *A. Horner, ed.*
(1-56821-212-7) $40.00 sc

Social Work

**Caring & Compassion in Clinical
Practice** *S. Sarason*
(1-56821-528-2) $40.00 sc

The Facilitating Partnership:
A Winnicottian Approach for Social Workers &
Other Helping Professionals *J. Applegate &
J. Bonovitz* (0-7657-0201-0) $30.00 sc

Fostering Healing & Growth:
A Psychoanalytic Social Work Approach
J. Edward & J. Sanville, eds.
(1-56821-723-4) $50.00

Inside Out and Outside In:
Psychodynamic Clinical Theory and Practice
in Contemporary Multicultural Contexts
J. Berzoff, L.M. Flanagan, & P. Hertz
(1-56821-777-3) $50.00

**Therapeutic Principles in Social
Work Practice:** A Primer for Clinicians
H.S. Strean (1-56821-137-6) $25.00 sc

Substance Abuse

**Couple and Family Therapy of
Addiction** *J.D. Levine*
(1-56821-641-6) $60.00

Coyote Speaks: Psychotherapy with
Alcoholics and Addicts *J. Rutzky*
(0-7657-0141-3) $40.00

**Creating the Capacity for
Attachment:** Treating Addictions and the
Alienated Self *K. Walant*
(0-7657-0240-1) $35.00 sc

**The Dynamics & Treatment of
Alcoholism** *J. Levin & R. Weiss, eds.*
(1-56821-072-8) $60.00

Gender & Addictions: Men & Women in
Treatment *S.L.A. Straussner & E. Zelvin, eds.*
(0-7657-0070-0) $65.00

Guidelines for Responsible Drinking
G. Forrest (1-56821-430-8) $30.00 sc

The Hidden Dimension *L. Wurmser*
(1-56821-591-6) $65.00 sc

Intensive Psychotherapy of Alcoholism *G. Forrest*
(1-56821-360-3) $45.00 sc

Liberating Solutions to Alcohol Problems *D. Cameron*
(1-56821-462-6) $50.00

Primer for Treating Substance Abusers *J.D. Levin* (0-7657-0078-6) $30.00

The Psychodynamics of Drug Dependence *J.D. Blaine & D.A. Julius*
(1-56821-157-0) $40.00 sc

Psychotherapy of Cocaine Addiction: Entering the Interpersonal World of the Cocaine Addict *D. Mark & J. Faude*
(0-7657-0072-7) $50.00

Recovery From Alcoholism *J. Levin*
(1-56821-186-4) $30.00 sc
(0-87668-625-0) $50.00

Substance-Abusing High Achievers: Addiction as an Equal Opportunity Destroyer *A.J. Twerski* (0-7657-0110-3) $30.00

Therapy of the Substance Abuse Syndromes *H. Richards*
(0-87668-539-4) $70.00

Treating Addiction as a Human Process *E.J. Khantzian*
(0-7657-0186-3) $70.00

Treatment of Abuse and Addiction: A Holistic Approach *A. Ciaramicoli*
(0-7657-0087-5) $50.00

Transference & Countertransference

The Analysis of the Transference in the Here & Now *G. Bauer*
(0-87668-143-7) $50.00

Beyond Countertransference *J. Natterson* (0-87668-558-0) $50.00

Countertransference *E. Slakter*
(0-87668-948-9) $50.00

Countertransference Enactment: How Institutions and Therapists Actualize Primitive Internal Worlds *R. Shur*
(1-56821-098-1) $50.00

Countertransference in Psychotherapy with Children and Adolescents *J.R. Brandell*
(0-7657-0281-9) $50.00 sc

Countertransference: The Therapist's Contribution to the Therapeutic Situation *L. Epstein & A. Feiner*
(1-56821-009-4) $60.00 sc

Countertransference Triumphs & Catastrophes *P. L. Giovacchini*
(0-87668-284-0) $60.00 sc

Counterresistance: The Therapist's Interference with the Therapeutic Process *G. Schoenewolf* (1-56821-079-5) $50.00

Essential Papers on Transference Analysis *G. Bauer, ed.*
(0-87668-529-7) $45.00 sc

Interpreting the Countertransference *L.E. Hedges*
(0-87668-532-7) $60.00

Love and Hate in the Analytic Setting *G. Gabbard* (0-7657-0291-6) $40.00 sc

Transference & Its Context: Selected Papers on Psychoanalysis *L. Stone*
(0-87668-655-2) $60.00

Transference Neurosis *M. Little*
(1-56821-074-4) $50.00 sc

The Uses of Countertransference *M. Gorkin* (1-56821-835-4) $50.00 sc

Winnicott

The Language of Winnicott: A Dictionary and Guide to Understanding His Work *J. Abram* (1-56821-700-5) $50.00

The Mind Object *E. Corrigan & P. Gordon* (1-56821-480-4) $50.00

In One's Bones: The Clinical Genius of Winnicott *D. Goldman*
(1-56821-020-5) $50.00 sc

In Search of the Real *D. Goldman*
(0-87668-006-6) $50.00

The Transitional Space *P. Giovacchini*
(1-56821-776-5) $50.00

The Work & Play of Winnicott
S. Grolnick (0-87668-802-4) $40.00

Women's Studies

Female Perversions *L.J. Kaplan*
(0-7657-0086-7) $35.00 sc